A Rhetoric of Divisive Partisanship

Lexington Studies in Political Communication

Series Editor: Robert E. Denton, Jr., Virginia Tech University

This series encourages focused work examining the role and function of communication in the realm of politics including campaigns and elections, media, and political institutions.

Titles in the Series

A Rhetoric of Divisive Partisanship

The 2016 American Presidential Campaign Discourse of Bernie Sanders and Donald Trump

Colleen Elizabeth Kelley

LEXINGTON BOOKS
Lanham • Boulder • New York • London

Published by Lexington Books
An imprint of The Rowman & Littlefield Publishing Group, Inc.
4501 Forbes Boulevard, Suite 200, Lanham, Maryland 20706
www.rowman.com

Unit A, Whitacre Mews, 26-34 Stannary Street, London SE11 4AB

British Library Cataloguing in Publication Information Available

Library of Congress Cataloging-in-Publication Data Available
Library of Congress Control Number: 2018931314

ISBN 978-1-4985-6457-1 (cloth : alk. paper)
ISBN 978-1-4985-6458-8 (electronic)

♾️™ The paper used in this publication meets the minimum requirements of American National Standard for Information Sciences Permanence of Paper for Printed Library Materials, ANSI/NISO Z39.48-1992.

Printed in the United States of America

To my sister Dana Marie Kelley

Contents

PREFACE

There have been recent calls for communication scholars to more actively embrace the civic nature and obligation of their discipline, as they discuss how to rebuild a sense of shared decency within a culture of evidence and fair debate in order to facilitate a publicly shared sense of justice. Studies within this research prototype ideally not only contribute to the discipline but also produce pragmatic results because such scholarship contributes to an enlightened, inclusive, reason-based paradigm of life within a constitutional democracy.

A Rhetoric of Divisive Partisanship: The 2016 American Presidential Campaign Discourse of Bernie Sanders and Donald Trump reaches beyond a traditional pedagogic frame in that it is situated within rhetoric, the theories of which informed democracy at its inception 2500 years ago and the practice of which is imperative for its survival into the twenty-first century. To that end, the book is conceived as both an act of disciplinary inquiry to further encourage scholarly conversations as well as a symbolic act of communication within the public sphere.

A Rhetoric of Divisive Partisanship would have been a different and diminished experience, both for the reader and writer, were it not for the colleagues, students, friends, and family who have contributed to a spirit of *ingenium* and bona fide hard work, both essentials for the completion of such a project. To that end, I wish to acknowledge two individuals by name. Echo Seiersen has been an astute and invaluable research assistant, signing on to this endeavor when it was only a series of questions and possibilities. She was instrumental in locating and evaluating a plethora of research monologues, transcripts, and archival material which ultimately coalesced into the exigence to which *A Rhetoric of Divisive Partisanship* responds. In addition, Ms. Seiersen's technical skills, patience, and attention to detail, through several revisions, are not only commendable but were essential to the completion of the book.

Finally, I wish to acknowledge the indefatigable enthusiasm and unwavering support offered by Miriam McMullen-Pastrick. For two decades, she was a formidable and insightful colleague as well as an exceptional and talented teacher and she remains a steadfast and beloved friend. Dr. McMullen-Pastrick possesses the most authentic sense of empathy and spirit of compassion I have ever encountered. I am forever indebted to her.

INTRODUCTION

Political communication is a crucial form of civic action, itself a prerequisite for a healthy democracy (Kendall-Taylor and Frantz 2016). Nowhere is this more evident than in the eighteen-month period leading up to the American presidential election on November 8, 2016. Informed by Burke's concepts of identification and division (1969), *A Rhetoric of Divisive Partisanship* extends the paradigm of divisive discourse to deconstruct the political rhetoric of Bernie Sanders and Donald Trump as they targeted ideologically different and affectively vulnerable constituencies during the 2016 presidential race. Sanders ran an effective campaign tapping the same anti-establishment fury Donald Trump stirred.

Although Sanders and Trump are very different, their campaigns were not. Each treated Hillary Clinton as a compromised, Wall Street–worshipping, Establishment sellout. Each appealed to marginalized segments of the electorate, albeit at opposite ends of the political spectrum, coalesced through a shared ideology grounded in antipolitics (Brooks 2016) rather than political or even party affiliation. Both polarized and reinforced their respective bases as "outsiders." Both relied on anti-establishment tropes and agent-centered scenarios of transformative power and perfection to create a shared, if unintentional, vision within which they joined their target audiences as marginalized outsiders united through a visceral disgust with and passion to overthrow the status quo and reclaim America.

In a sense, each represented "the same phenomenon in reverse" (Goldberg 2015). Despite their avowed "right" and "left" rhetorical stances, Bernie Sanders and Donald Trump shared a number of policy positions. Each opposed the Trans-Pacific Partnership trade agreement, supported Social Security benefits, endorsed tax hikes, condemned the role of money in politics, and opposed the Iraq war. In addition, both agreed that increased immigration could threaten American workers, supported single-payer health care, vacillated on gun control and shared common ground in their desire to defeat Hillary Clinton.

This text expands on previous theoretical approaches to dialogue and political rhetoric and argues that rather than serving as a paradigm of civic and civil discourse, the rhetoric of Sanders and Trump was reactionary and intentionally divisive, albeit instigated with different intentions and producing different results, none of which leaned in the direction of consensus building or deliberative discourse, both rhetorically based prerequisites for effective and ethical participation in American government. It then argues that such rhetorical forms, which exist on a populist-to-fascist continuum, have not only become global phenomena, but more significantly are likely to be foregrounded in future American political races. This is significant in that such rhetorical behaviors not only inform the norms and practices of democratically elected leaders, but also stabilize and enable constitutional democracies, including that which still survives in the United States.

A Rhetoric of Divisive Partisanship argues that the 2016 presidential campaign was strategically orchestrated to privilege division over consensus to assuage Sanders's and Trump's allegedly abandoned and decidedly angry publics. Significantly, both did so with negligible efforts to confront or accept responsibility for the formidable threat their campaigns posed to American's shared liberties. The book concludes speculatively, suggesting an egalitarian yet affectively visceral and classically rhetorical model to unify rather than divide populist and partisan democracies—including that of the United States—to counter what, particularly in a "post-truth" era of incivility and uncertainly, is likely to be an increased reliance on ethically suspect but decidedly effective discursive behaviors.

ONE

A Rhetoric of Divisive Partisanship

Bernie Sanders's campaign style has been compared to Obama in 2008, Reagan in 1980, Bobby Kennedy in 1968, and John Kennedy in 1960. "That's Sanders in a nutshell" in that "such candidates catch "Zeitgeist in a bottle"; they "have not voters, but believers, receive not support, but faith" (Pitts, Jr. 2016). On many major issues—including the signature issues of his 2016 campaign, especially financial reform—he seemed to go for easy slogans over "hard thinking." And his political theory of change, his waving away of limits, seemed to some unrealistic. "Some Sanders supporters responded angrily when these concerns were raised, immediately accusing anyone expressing doubts about their hero of being corrupt if not actually criminal" (Krugman 2016c).

Donald Trump's June 2015 declaration of his candidacy for the Republican nomination was initially treated as a joke, with the candidate polling at one percent in pre-primary polls. However, by the summer of 2016, he had "pulled off one of the greatest political coups in modern history, defeating sixteen other candidates—including governors and senators—to become the GOP's nominee for president" by riding a middle-aged white, working-class "wave of anger" (Packer quoted in *GOP: How Trump Defied*, 2016).

More than 57.6 million people, or 28.5 percent of estimated eligible voters, voted in the Republican and Democratic presidential primaries that wrapped up in June 2016—close to but not quite at the record participation level set in 2008 (Desilver 2016). Donald Trump got more votes in a Republican nominating contest than anyone on record. The previous record for most votes for a Republican in the primaries was held by George W. Bush in 2000. However, Trump also had more votes against him. The giant field of Republican candidates meant that votes in the early primaries were split widely, making it hard for anyone

1

to cobble together a majority. It also appears to have meant that more people came out to vote. So, it's not a surprise that Trump also set a record for the most votes cast against the top vote-getter—or that he won a lower percentage of votes than anyone since Reagan in 1968 (Bump 2016d).

King (2016) reports that while Trump got a lot of attention for drawing new voters into the GOP primaries, his total vote tally—13.3 million votes—fell well below Democratic challenger and eventual nominee Hillary Clinton's votes. In addition, his numbers were diluted because he faced more than a dozen challengers. And by May 2016, it appeared difficult for Bernie Sanders and his supporters to acknowledge that "'the Bern' had all but burned itself out" (Pitts, Jr. 2016). Ultimately, "Clinton won 16.8 million votes to 13.2 million for Sanders, or about 55 percent of the vote to his 43 percent" (Silver 2016). A month later, Hillary Clinton and Donald Trump had become the nominees of their respective parties for the 2016 presidential race.

SITUATING ANTI-ESTABLISHMENT DISCOURSE

It has generally always been politically expedient to fight the establishment. Insurgent conservatives like Barry Goldwater in the mid-twentieth century used to rail against the "Eastern establishment," which implied an elitist, Ivy League and (implicitly) hail-fellow style. Goldwater was anti-establishment in the early 1960s, as was Ronald Reagan. They built robust followings. Goldwater wound up winning the Republican presidential nomination in 1964, and Reagan ascended to the presidency in 1980, injecting their brands of conservatism into the core of the Republican establishment. Likewise, Bill Clinton and Barack Obama both ran for president as "Washington outsiders," which suggested anti-establishment credibility. But living in the White House carries with it a lifetime membership in the establishment, with little opportunity for escape. Recent conditions have fostered a particularly lethal stigma against their breed. Grass-roots movements like the Tea Party, Occupy Wall Street, and social media (mainly Twitter and Facebook) have energized resistance to the vague establishment. Super PACs have placed huge amounts of political money into the hands of people far removed from the party operatives who used to control the coffers (Leibovich 2016).

Rhetorical Positioning of Sanders and Trump

Anti-establishment sentiments dominated the discussion of the 2016 election. Both Sanders and Trump rhetorically differentiated and split their respective segments of voters from the Democratic and Republican mainstream. While initially more evident on the right with the rise of

Donald Trump, they became increasingly more apparent on the left, with support for Bernie Sanders (Geiger 2016). Both the Vermont democratic socialist and the New York billionaire took advantage of disenfranchised grassroots movements as well as a "fight the establishment" ethos and positioned themselves as outsiders who could rescue their segments of an "orphaned electorate" from the mainstream and protect their constituents from self-serving, out-of-touch, and grossly incompetent politicians. Both Trump and Sanders rhetorically situated mainstream politicians in their respective and newly adopted parties as ill-prepared, wrong-headed, and narcissistic charlatans:

> To be part of the establishment is most certainly a bad look in today's politics. It represents a catchall designation for "people in charge" — and implies that they've been ensconced too long. The establishment is tired and musty and too comfortable (Leibovich 2016).

Both outsider candidates framed their core supporters, representing the two extremes of the American "conservative-to-liberal" political spectrum, as victims of the establishment in need of rescuing by Donald Trump, as the "savior of the Right" and Bernie Sanders, as the "savior of the Left." In the politics of 2016, Donald Trump and Bernie Sanders were the "party crashers" while mainstream politicians such as Jeb Bush and Hillary Clinton were configured as "the fuddy-duddy neighborhood-association types" so that "no shortage of contempt" was "reserved for them" (Leibovich 2016).

For the Democrats, Barack Obama's ascent to the presidency was often tied to his message of hope and change, yet his short political resume may have played a far more critical role than many recognize. Strong support for self-proclaimed socialist Bernie Sanders seemed to demonstrate the same anti-establishment sentiments among Democrats that likely helped propel then first-term Senator Obama to the presidency over establishment favorite Hillary Clinton (Geiger 2016). Barack Obama and Bernie Sanders both personified the very notion of anti-establishment. Where the right has targeted government overreach and spending, the left sees special interests and their undue influence on the government that comes at the expense of the American people as the most pressing threat (Geiger 2016).

THE APPEAL OF THE POPULIST UNDERDOG

In May of 2016, *Miami Herald* columnist Leonard Pitts, Jr., wrote "the extreme left now mirrors the extreme right, each reflecting the anger and unbending rigidity of the other" and that both Donald Trump and Bernie Sanders sounded "like the kid who snatches his ball and storms out of the park after losing a game" (2016). *Washington Post* columnist Michael

Gerson argues that Bernie Sanders and Donald Trump were both self-styled populists who considered themselves revolutionaries but were both "in fact, backward-looking, intellectually timid and unresponsive to the real needs of the working and middle classes" (2016). Many in the Sanders and Trump camps considered politics a "reflection of career disappointments" including some from among the nearly five million Americans who had lost jobs in manufacturing since 2000, or the millions of white-collar workers who had lost jobs due to shifts in technology or employer preferences for younger workers (Carney 2016).

This underdog appeal informed both campaigns. Wertheim and Sommers (2016) suggest Americans "want the little guys to triumph" or "at least we think they do." To illustrate, researchers at Bowling Green State documented the phenomenon. They told more than 100 survey respondents that Team A was playing Team B in a best-of-seven series in an unspecified sport. Team A was highly favored to win. Which would they root for? Eighty-one percent said the underdog. But then the subjects were told that Team B, the underdog, had, improbably, taken a 3–0 lead in the series. Now which team would they support? Half switched over to Team A, the original favorite, but now the squad on the verge of elimination.

An additional study revealed that underdog status does not only inspire rooting, it also changes observer's perception of what is seen on the court. When told that a team was the underdog, research participants saw a play like a defender getting close to an opponent and knocking the ball away as reflecting hustle and grit. When watching the very same play, but under the impression that it came from the favored team instead, people saw the tough defense as more of a reflection of natural ability, not effort.

Politicians "know this too." Many discursively establish an "underdog" ethos that situates them "in a log cabin" which, as with a sports team, produces "emotional payoff":

> There's more potential for return on the investment when you root for the underdog than when the expected happens and the favorite wins. We get such a surge from seeing upsets, and cheering for the least likely outcome, that we're willing to risk the lesser odds. But perhaps most of all, we're drawn to the message that giants can be toppled, that with a little luck we, too, can overcome (Wertheim and Sommers 2016).

Bernie Sanders campaigned to be the "first Jewish president" while Donald Trump "presumably would have decorated that log cabin with . . . his own name and logo in gaudy gold lettering" and so framed his campaign "through the lens of outsider cachet" (Wertheim and Sommers 2016).

POPULIST APPEALS THROUGH SOCIAL MEDIA

Both Bernie Sanders and Donald Trump engaged in effective populist rhetoric, a type of discourse with an essential idea which "resides in a representation of or acting in the name of ordinary or common people and masses and opposing those elites, privileged groups, the establishment, etc." (Latifi 2015). Both of these "outsider" candidates enacted their primary campaigns as a sort of "direct democracy" via social media. And both incessantly and effectively utilized social network platforms such as Reddit, Facebook, and Twitter to secure and maintain ideological conduits between themselves as political actors and their "disenfranchised" portions of the electorate "in a direct way, rather than mediated through organizations or media outlets" (Latifi 2015).

The Media as Enabler

An analysis by the Harvard Kennedy School's Shorenstein Center on Media, Politics and Public Policy of news coverage from the 2016 primary races found that mainstream media outlets engaged in "journalistic bias" which resulted in over-coverage of the Donald Trump campaign and under-coverage of Democratic candidates, in particular Senator Bernie Sanders (Patterson 2016a). The study underscores the role that the press can play in anointing—or sinking—a candidate, as well as keeping voters under-informed by focusing only on the horse race instead of the candidates or relevant issues. It also highlights how the press helped to elevate Trump while contributing to the downfall of rival candidates, and paid relatively little attention to the Democratic nominating contest.

For the report, a content analysis firm, Media Tenor, examined statements from CBS, Fox, the *Los Angeles Times, NBC*, the *New York Times, USA Today*, the *Wall Street Journal*, and the *Washington Post.* "Game-centered reporting has consequences," the report said. "The media's tendency to allocate coverage based on winning and losing affects voters' decisions. The press's attention to early winners, and its tendency to afford them more positive coverage than their competitors, is not designed to boost their chances, but that's a predictable effect." The press does not favor certain candidates because it is engaged in a vast conspiracy, according to the report. It's a lot simpler: reporters like a good story. It's what their business is based on. And in 2016, Trump's narrative seemed more novel than that of Clinton or Sanders.

This isn't the first time the press has "fallen for a candidate." Barack Obama received "outsized coverage" when he first ran in 2008, as did Senator John McCain in 2000, when he invited reporters aboard his campaign bus, the "Straight Talk Express." Trump, the report said, is now on that list. The press's extensive focus on the horse race also leaves less time for substantive coverage, the report said. Mainstream media primary

coverage was almost entirely about the competition or the campaign process. By comparison, only eleven percent of the primary coverage focused
on the candidates' policy positions, leadership abilities, or personal and
professional histories. "Substantive concerns got the least amount of attention," the report found—on both sides of the aisle.

Even before the primaries began, Trump dominated media coverage.
As he continued to win primaries, his story became about gaining momentum, a narrative that held fast. "Victory for Trump was also his path
to positive coverage," the report said. Senator Marco Rubio, by contrast,
was portrayed as consistently losing ground after he failed to win an
early contest. Rubio never had, the report said, "a single week where his
positive press outpaced his negative press." Trump did receive more
substantive coverage in the final month of the campaign, when there
were no other competitors in the Republican race, the report said. References to his character and policies rose from 10 percent to 19 percent, and
the tone was overwhelmingly negative. Ultimately, the report attributed
Trump's candidacy in part to the coverage. "He might have won the
Republican nomination in any case, given the confluence of factors working in his favor," it said. "But one of his assets, certainly, was his press
advantage."

On the Democratic side, the candidates generally received coverage
on par with their primary results: Clinton received 54 percent of the press
attention, versus Sanders's 46 percent, until the middle stage of the campaign—mid-March to early May—when Clinton pulled ahead. Sanders
also received more positive media attention—the largest favorable margin of any candidate, 59 percent good press to 41 percent bad press—
until the middle stage of the campaign, the report found.

Critical Media Coverage

At the same time, reports on Clinton were more critical because as the
presumptive nominee, she was expected by the press to dominate the
early contests. By the middle stage of the campaign, however, Clinton
was eking out more favorable press, 51 percent positive to 49 percent
negative. But once she clinched the nomination, she received more criticism, with 49 percent positive statements to 51 percent negative, in part
because Trump began to target her in speeches. However, no matter what
the Democratic candidates did, the Republican contest continued to dominate the press coverage, even when Trump became the presumptive
nominee. "Although Trump no longer had active opposition, he received
more news coverage in the last month than did either Clinton or Sanders," the report said, "a development that has no possible explanation
other than journalistic bias" (Childress 2016).

DeCosta-Klipa (2016) also references the Shorenstein study in his es-
say about the media coverage of Trump, Sanders, and Clinton. The Sand-

ers campaign had complained about the "Bernie Blackout," during his campaign, arguing that the media had "ignored" them relative to the coverage given to other candidates. The anti-Sanders bent, Sanders argued, was not just quantitative, but also qualitative with the corporate-owned media inherently biased against the slate of issues his "revolution" embraced.

The Harvard analysis reveals that Sanders was right in his critique—and also wrong. While Sanders's ability to gain traction nationally early on was hurt by the media's obsession with the Republican side of the race, less coverage of the Democratic side worked against his efforts to make inroads on Clinton's support. Sanders struggled to get badly needed press attention early in the campaign cycle. By summer, Sanders had emerged as Clinton's leading competitor but, even then, his coverage lagged. Not until the pre-primary debates did his coverage begin to pick up, though not at a rate close to what he needed to compensate for the early part of the year.

The study found that five Republican candidates—Trump, Jeb Bush, Ted Cruz, Marco Rubio, and Ben Carson—each got more coverage than Sanders during 2015 and that Clinton herself received three times as much press as did the Vermont senator. According to those findings, Sanders would appear to be justified in his complaint about coverage quantity. It is significant that, with regards to the substance of that coverage, at least over the course of 2015, Sanders was on less solid ground and was actually the most favorably reported candidate—Republican or Democratic—during the "invisible primary" of 2015. Once his campaign launched, the study found the tone "shot into positive territory" before falling in October. The study attributes the slip to Sanders performance in the debates; October was also the time that the Clinton and Sanders campaigns first began openly attacking one another. Even when it came to the issues, which Sanders chastised the media for ignoring, his policies were a source of good news for the campaign, despite being a small percentage of his total coverage. From the study:

> News statements about Sanders' stands on income inequality, the mini-mum wage, student debt, and trade agreements were more than three-to-one positive over negative. That ratio far exceeded those of other top candidates, Republican or Democratic (DeCosta-Kilpa 2016).

FOUNDERS' CONCERNS ABOUT DEMOCRACY

Donald Trump and Bernie Sanders waged an essentially united primary campaign against Hillary Clinton, driven by their shared ethos as outsiders and their shared audience of disaffected and volatile Americans. Each rhetorically captured the "will of the people" and condemned any person or idea or project which could be framed as a violation of that will. They may have also collaborated through an archetypal twenty-first century antipolitical and pathos-driven campaign discourse. This is not a new concern. Trees (2016) maintains that "the Founding Fathers" in the eighteenth century were "far more worried about a demagogue seizing power than they were about following the voice of the people." They intended the election of the president to be well-insulated from a direct expression of the popular will:

> They were far more worried about too much democracy than they were about too little democracy [because] they did not entirely trust the people, who were too likely to be ruled by passion rather than guided by reason. As James Madison wrote, "It is a misfortune, inseparable from human affairs, that public measures are rarely investigated with that spirit of moderation which is essential to a just estimate of their real tendency to advance or obstruct the public good; and that their spirit is more apt to be diminished than promoted by those occasions which require an unusual exercise of it" (Trees 2016).

Trees (2016) comments on the 2016 primary campaign in light of this view, noting that "no one would argue that [a] 'spirit of moderation' has presided" over the primaries and that, "much as Madison and the other Founders feared, passion instead of reason is the driving force this election cycle."

Williamson (2016) argues a major concern of John Adams about eighteenth-century democracy was the unfettered "passion" of Americans and recalls Adams's assessment of that concern:

> Democracy has never been and never can be so durable as aristocracy or monarchy; but while it lasts, it is more bloody than either. . . . It soon wastes, exhausts, and murders itself. There never was a democracy yet that did not commit suicide. It is in vain to say that democracy is less vain, less proud, less selfish, less ambitious, or less avaricious than aristocracy or monarchy. It is not true, in fact, and nowhere appears in history. Those passions are the same in all men, under all forms of simple government, and when unchecked, produce the same effects of fraud, violence, and cruelty (quoted in Williamson 2016).

"Trumpkin democracy," according to Williamson (2016), is the democracy that John Adams warned about. At some point within the past few decades (it is difficult to identify the exact genesis) the rhetorical affectation of politicians' presuming to speak for "We the People" became fashionable. Donald Trump's vision of an imperial presidency embodies the fears that "kept John Adams up at night":

> A proper republic under the rule of law is, as Adams wrote, "deaf as an adder to the clamors of the populace." It is that which "no passion can disturb" and "void of desire and fear, lust and anger," being, as it is, "mens sine affectu." The Trump movement is light on the mens, being almost entirely affectu.

In this view, Bernie Sanders's campaign rhetoric was as troublesome as Trump's because both were driven primarily by "democratic passion" at the expense of more substantive discursive strategies. To illustrate, while laws including those of property, trade, and individual rights are situated within America's constitutional democracy, they—along with First Amendment rights and unpopular viewpoints—are rejected or ignored. Just as during John Adams's lifetime, the darkest aspects of human nature are exaggerated by the liberal character of American institutions. In Adams's words:

> [But] should the people of America once become capable of that deep simulation towards one another, and towards foreign nations, which assumes the language of justice and moderation, while it is practising iniquity and extravagance, and displays in the most grin rapine and insolence, this country will be the most miserable habitation in the world. Because we have no government, armed with power, capable of contending with human passions. . . . Avarice, ambition, revenge and licentiousness would break the strongest cords of our Constitution [which is] wholly inadequate to the government of any other. Oaths in this country are as yet universally considered as sacred obligations . . . the federal character of the United States, and the fractured nature of the federal government . . . are designed to frustrate 'We the People' when the people fall into dangerous and violent error of the sort with which they are now flirting (quoted in Williamson 2016).

VOTER KNOWLEDGE BASE

It may be argued the American electorate does not have adequate knowledge for voters to control public policy. Scholars have long documented the limits of voter knowledge about the institutions and policies of the government. That ignorance is not necessarily a moral failing in that a rational—albeit ill-informed or uninformed—voter has little incentive to gain more knowledge about politics because his or her vote is unlikely to affect the outcome. Inadequate voter knowledge prevents government from reflecting the will of the people in any meaningful way. Such ignorance also raises doubts about democracy as a means of serving the interests of a majority. In addition, voters who lack sufficient knowledge may be manipulated by elites and may also demand policies that contravene their own interests (Somin 2004). Hochschild (2010) reports that "most every democratic theorist or democratic political actor sees an informed electorate as essential to good democratic practice." As a result, it is imperative that citizens "know who or what they are choosing and why," hence the need for leaders to demand funded education, and rights to free speech, assembly, press, and movement.

The persistent angry agitation rhetoric of popular leaders such as Sanders and Trump, who defaulted to divisive rather than bipartisan messaging, does not constitute either a robust or a healthy discursive environment within which to situate American politics. This is primarily because a working democracy—including that of the United States—is sustained through leadership which maintains an infrastructure and produces the literal speech necessary to sustain a system through which the public is consistently informed. In this manner, and as "imperfect" as the ideal of an "informed electorate" may be, the pragmatic functionalism of a democratic nation driven by a popular opinion may continue to exist.

Appeals to "Citizens in the Mass"

In sum, Bernie Sanders and Donald Trump, as they enacted Campaign 2016, embraced an "impresario of the mob" ethos as they simultaneously framed their audiences within similar rhetorical contexts. Their disenfranchised liberal-left /conservative-right audiences were constituted as outsiders, abandoned by mainstream politicians and in need of nothing less than a political revolution, each driven by their respective "outsider" leaders.

DIVISIVE PARTISANSHIP TEAMWORK AS A RHETORICAL STRATEGY

The idea that American politics is the "art of compromise, where everybody gets something" is an artifact "from a distant age" (Pitts, Jr. 2016). In one sense, the rhetorical appeals Bernie Sanders and Donald Trump directed at their disenfranchised segment of the electorate fit into the canon of "rhetorical agency," specifically as related to "ownership" of rhetoric and "legitimate performances of rhetoric" (Waite 2012). In this configuration "outsider" discourse is situated within a broader category of "otherness" (see Stockdell-Giesler 2010). While their respective target audiences occupied opposite ends of the political spectrum (Trump's conservative Republican base was primarily disillusioned and angry white working-class men while Sanders's liberal Democratic base was primarily idealistic college-educated and angry white millennials), both candidates relied on powerful and successful appeals located within an "otherness."

CNN analyst Fareed Zakaria observed in March 2016 that "the energy fueling the presidential campaign on both sides of the political spectrum seems to be deep despair about the American economy" and that "on this central issue, Bernie Sanders and Donald Trump shared a surprisingly similar message." One *New York Times* letter-to-the-editor contributor demanded that Bernie Sanders "wake up" and called on the Democratic candidate to back away from his fervent anti-globalization stance for the United States as it could help elect Donald Trump. Furthermore, the writer continued, Sanders's aggressive push for a protectionist agenda and his continuing refusal to accept Democratic primary results offered additional support for Mr. Trump's campaign against Clinton and an endorsement of the Republican's use "of the very same rhetoric" (Ho 2016). Another writer corroborated a concern about Sanders's possible collusion with Trump and cautioned that Sanders:

> must stop his largely egomaniacal attitude toward Hillary Clinton and the Democratic Party before he damaged his own revolution. A Donald Trump win, which Mr. Sanders in now dangerously helping, would end his political revolution for good and for certain (Wickens 2016).

Bernie Sanders and Donald Trump "double-teamed" Clinton's candidacy in that both discursively created, reinforced, and embellished perceptions of abandonment in their respective target audiences through a discourse of divisive partisanship. Ultimately, this rhetorical mechanism so successfully created an "angry orphan" persona in both candidates' segments of a marginalized and affectively vulnerable electorate that they united to decimate the ethos of Hillary Clinton, possibly delivering the fatal blow to her campaign. The outcome of this unorthodox partnership was that one member (an outsider with a thirty-year history of socialism and non-party affiliation) came close to being his party's nominee while the other (an outsider with a thirty-year history of extreme wealth, investments, and political party opportunism) became a president of the United States.

TWO

"Other" / "Outsider" Rhetoric

Anti-establishment "outsider" discourse dominated the 2016 presidential election. The twin campaigns of Bernie Sanders and Donald Trump were paradigms of this rhetoric as illustrated by mirrored populist campaigns, both of which tapped into many of the same public sentiments. Characteristics of this shared ideology included a deep suspicion of political, corporate, and media élites; an eagerness to mobilize people who were new to politics; and a willingness to embrace policies that have long seemed forbidden (Cassidy 2016). And while frequently more obvious "on the right with the rise of Donald Trump" it was "also apparent on the left, with support for Bernie Sanders" (Geiger 2016). This is because voters were increasingly disenchanted by the political process and, more specifically, politicians. The unpopularity of career politicians has set the stage for the rise of a new class of political outsiders and a particular popularity for the candidates who "speak extemporaneously, shoot from the hip and buck the Washington establishment at every turn" (Madden 2015; see also Rauch 2015 and Stid 2014).

> Voters appear committed to shutting out professional politicians [and] believe the system is corrupt and rigged against them to benefit political elites on both sides of the aisle. . . . This frustration with the direction of the country and disdain for establishment politics has opened the door for outsider candidates to dominate the playing field like never before (Madden 2015).

PRECEDENTS IN AMERICAN POLITICS

This is not an entirely unique behavior for the American public. Busch (1997) tracks the origin of "outsider" American presidential candidates to the early 1870s and identifies the Prohibitionists, Populists, Barry Gold-

13

water, Jimmy Carter, Jesse Jackson, Ross Perot, Pat Buchanan, Steve Forbes, and David Duke as quintessential outsider candidates. In this view, an outsider candidate is one who is outside the corridors of power, in the sense either of holding no office or of residing outside the "mainstream "or majority of the party, explicitly rejecting the party's leadership and dominant element; serves as the spokesperson or representative of a broader group (a political movement) outside the corridors of power; and/or serves as the spokesman or representative of ideas, ideologies, or themes that challenge the dominant element in the party" (2).

Busch attributes the "explosion of outsiderism" in American politics to several factors. First, the theme of outsiderism was a utilitarian frame and so became more useful. Second, it became more common as candidates created perceptions of themselves as outsiders. Finally, outsiderism was framed in unconventional ways, when unconnected outsiders found support from organized movements (152–153). Janack (2006) suggests that among the most successful of these political outsiders was Jesse "The Body" Ventura in his campaign for and occupation of Minnesota's governorship. Drawing on Mikhail Bakhtin's concept of carnival (see Bakhtin 1941), Janack suggests that Ventura's discourse and symbolic action contained carnivalesque references and images. Such references contributed to his image as a political outsider and associated him with the carnival fool's role of protest against the prevailing political system.

In September, 2002, novelist and journalist Anna Quindlen suggested that family members of those murdered on September 11, 2001, could potentially become effective political leaders (Janack 2006). Quindlen believed the moral authority endowed by tragedy upon the families of those who died in the September 2001 American terrorist attacks, enabled the survivors to become the "vox populi" and lead in ways that contemporary American elected officials never could. The 2016 presidential campaign, as collaboratively performed by Bernie Sanders and Donald Trump, suggests that quintessential political outsiders have found their own voice as the country's "vox populi," through identification with a disenfranchised, partisan, and angry American public. Furthermore, theirs was a rhetorical act grounded in strategies of division and unity, the result of which was Donald Trump's election as president.

RHETORIC AND CONSUBSTANTIALITY

Identification as Method

Edelman (1988) notes that language is not merely a tool for describing objective reality, but the key creator of the social worlds people experience (103). This premise undergirds much of rhetorical theory, including the works of Kenneth Burke who considers symbolic action the primary means with which humans influence the world and each other (1966). Burke (1969) considers "identification" to be the key term of rhetoric and an extension of the traditional term "persuasion." It is a process fundamental to being a human and communicating as a human. Because humans are biologically separate from one another, they want to identify with others in order to assuage their natural state of isolation. They look for ways in which interests, attitudes, values, experiences, perceptions, and material properties are shared with others, or could be shared. In so doing, people become "consubstantial" with one another; their "substances" or essences overlap so that identification bridges differences between human beings. Understanding the process of identification facilitates an understanding of the processes with which people build social cohesion through language. In this sense, language is symbolic action, a way of acting in the world that is purposeful and that conveys attitudes (41). Humans connect with one another through shared experiences or goals:

> A is not identical with his colleague, B. But insofar as their interests are joined, A is *identified* with B. Or he may *identify himself* with B even when their interests are not joined, if he assumes that they are, or is persuaded to believe so (Burke 1990, 1020).

Three primary types of processes or states of identification include: (1) naming something (or someone) according to specific properties; (2) the process of associating with and disassociating from others; and (3) the end result of identifying: being consubstantial with others. The process of identification can be achieved through "speech, gesture, tonality, order, image, attitude, and idea" (Burke 1931, 136). Sharing with leaders or spokespersons is a potent form of identification (Burke 1990). In traditional terms, association may be explicit; "a speaker persuades an audience by the use of stylistic identifications" so that the "act of persuasion may be for the purpose of causing the audience to identify itself with the speaker's interests" (1969, 46). The individual and partisan rhetorical assaults of Sanders and Trump ultimately converged their supporters into a unified and angry front, seeking vindication, if not salvation, through voting for each man against "her."

Divisive Populism as Strategy of Unification

Timothy McCarthy, an historian of political and social movements at Harvard University's Kennedy School of Government, argues that America's political polarization was being fueled by growing economic inequality, on the one hand, and rising social ignorance, on the other. This polarization was typified by Bernie Sanders and Donald Trump. On the "left," Bernie Sanders's democratic socialism spoke to widespread discontent with capitalism as well as corporate control of politics while

Trump's "right" appeal made an equally forceful case for a more conservative—even reactionary—policy agenda. Both spoke to "darker forces of fear and prejudice that exist in America" and both appeal to the "good and the bad" of populist sentiment which drew huge crowds and even bipartisan support (quoted in Ross 2015).

Both men targeted essentially the same base: Americans who felt threatened by a disappearing middle class. However, each base feared the erosion of the middle class for different reasons. While Trump played to "people who have the least" as those most threatened, Sanders directed his campaign at "the people who have the most" (*Top Takeaways from Nevada,* 2016).

OUTSIDER SELF-IDENTIFICATION

Ciruli (2016) speculates whether twenty-first century Western democracies are facing an existential crisis and suggests that a global anger and frustration fuels what may be an historic challenge to political and party establishments. This was exemplified by the 2016 US presidential campaign trail, where political outsiders rode "a wave of voter discontent." These candidates, some with little or no political experience, were previously discounted as "unelectable." However, in the election cycle which culminated in the January 2017 ascension of Donald Trump to the American presidency, voters seemed "more interested in an opportunity to vent than the traditional calculus of electability."

When former Florida governor Jeb Bush announced his candidacy in June 15, 2015, his advisors believed his major challenge for winning the White House was to separate himself from the troubled record of his brother concerning Iraq. However, "he didn't have long to savor his status as the establishment favorite" when, the next day, Donald Trump entered the race with "signature bluster" ultimately obliterating other Republicans including Senators Ted Cruz and Marco Rubio. While they and other "traditional" Republicans were "mad as hell" at things as usual, it was Trump's announcement—including his statement that Mexico is sending people that have "lots of problems" to America and he was going to "build a great wall"—that electrified the angry Republican voter, changing the race and possibly American politics for the foreseeable future.

ELECTORATE ANGER

Electorate anger, on both sides of the aisle, fueled the campaigns of both Bernie Sanders and Donald Trump. Each embraced an "anti-establishment"/un-politician ethos and together rode "a wave of populist support rooted in voters' anger at the political status quo" (Dickinson 2015). Each time Trump survived or benefitted from a "politically incorrect" viewpoint, he shifted the course of the Republican race in his direction. His attacks included issue and personal assaults on immigration, John McCain, Megyn Kelly, and Muslims which helped him to "tap into a rage" among voters who insisted they were just waiting for someone to "tell it like it is." Democrats also witnessed a challenge to the trajectory of their expected presidential campaign shift. To illustrate, although Hillary Clinton generally maintained her front-runner status, the race cumulatively became more competitive than expected, with Bernie Sanders's passionate appeals successfully gaining support among Barack Obama's young and liberal constituents who prefer his anti-Wall Street, anti-K Street rhetoric (Ciruli 2016).

Sanders and Trump as Saviors

Original American populists in the 1890s perceived themselves as champions of "common citizens" by channeling fears and frustrations of Southern and Midwestern farmers who were straining to keep up in an increasingly industrialized and national economy. In a real sense, these "little people" were the nineteenth century's "orphaned" electorate, a segment of Americans who became increasingly resentful toward an emerging twentieth-century culture that no longer venerated them but rather pandered to corporations. As a result, they advocated extending government power to regulate capitalism and "big business" in order to relieve the debt burden of the "little people," and to destroy the profiteers who threatened not only their livelihood but their way of life:

> Perhaps ironically, populism—including that represented by appeals from candidates from the entire 2016 political spectrum— evolved from the economic and cultural dispossession of "little people," in particular a subset for whom populists seldom speak: ethnic minorities and African-Americans, historically among the most undervalued as well as economically and culturally dispossessed in the nation. Original populists were largely inhospitable if not hostile to the millions of blacks and immigrants living in America at the time, reflecting the worldview of their Southern and Midwestern base and an abiding nativism that permeated much of the movement (Steinhorn 2017).

Two Candidates: One Ethos

By inadvertently uniting their campaigns through mirrored rhetorical positioning of themselves as "outsiders," Bernie Sanders and Donald Trump were seen as "going rogue," if not together then at least the same direction (Leibovich 2016). Toynbee (2016) asserts that Hillary Clinton arrived in the "pole position" as a presidential contender, accompanied by a "searing firestorm of abuse from both Bernie Sanders and Donald

Trump, with hotter blowtorches to come." Like Trump, Sanders also included profanity in his political discourse, albeit in a more "proper" manner: his "damn in connection with wanting to hear no more about Hillary
Clinton's email was righteously indignant and an obvious exception to
the way he usually speaks" (quoted in Ross 2015).

To illustrate, like Trump, Sanders framed American policies as being
hijacked by special interests. He consistently argued the 2008–2009 financial crisis was foisted on average working Americans by American bankers whose self-interest almost destroyed the American economy:

> The sad reality is that the Federal Reserve doesn't regulate Wall Street;
> Wall Street regulates the Fed. It's time to make banking work for the
> productive economy and for all Americans, not just a handful of
> wealthy speculators. . . . If Congress cannot regulate Wall Street, there
> is just one alternative. It is time to break these too-big-to-fail banks up
> so that they can never again destroy the jobs, homes, and life savings of
> the American people (quoted in Mahbubani 2016).

Troy Campbell, a University of Oregon professor of marketing, concludes that substantial segments of Trump's and Sanders's orphaned
electorates shared concerns which drew them to candidates with a
"change-preaching, anti-Washington, entertaining, take-no prisoners,
apologize-for-nothing personality." Such voters increasingly became less
identified with "a" party and more generally with "the" antipolitical establishment. It was this anti-political-elite sentiment which ran deep in
both the Sanders and Trump constituencies (Campbell quoted in Edsall
2016).

Shared Issues

Roberts and Roberts (2016b) note the disillusionment with politics and
government now plaguing the election process has been badly aggravat-
ed by politicians in both parties making promises they "knew they could
not keep." This trend was exemplified by Donald Trump's claims including vowing to deport eleven million undocumented immigrants and Bernie Sanders's insistence that he would bring about a "political revolution" and so forever change the landscape of American government.
While "easy and extreme slogans"—like "Expel the foreigners!" or "Soak
the billionaires!"—which were connected to their respective campaigns,
made great bumper stickers and applause lines, both were virtually use-
less guides for governing the country, which:

> requires accommodation, not anger; determination, not delusion. . . .
> But [Trump's] idea . . . that undocumented immigrants can somehow
> be seized and sent home, is totally impractical and morally reprehen-
> sible. That policy would rip apart millions of families while undermin-
> ing key sectors of the economy. Thousands of jobs, many of them in the

service sector, would simply go undone . . . these proposals play on the worst phobias that always lurk just below the surface of American life: the fear of "others," the irrational and ignorant belief that America is now perfect and the next wave of newcomers will somehow deface and degrade our culture. . . . Sanders's proposal for a hugely expensive, government-run program of universal coverage is equally unsustainable. President Barack Obama used every ounce of political capital to push through a much more modest program of expanded health insurance, and even then failed to attract a single Republican vote. . . . [His] self-regarding analysis implies a national consensus favoring his agenda when there is none and ignores the many legitimate checks and balances in the political system that he cannot wish away (Roberts and Roberts 2016b).

"The numbers don't remotely add up," concludes Austan Goolsbee, formerly Obama's chief economic adviser (cited in Roberts and Roberts, 2016b).

Some have also argued that Sanders and Trump both indulged in economic, if not different, fantasies. Republicans have "routinely" advocated "deep voodoo" with claims about the positive effects. In May 2016 Trump advocated reducing the "current" seven tax brackets to four and cutting the top rate on the wealthy to 25 percent, from 39.6 percent. He also called for eliminating the estate tax, which affects only the very wealthy with more than $5.45 million in assets at death, and the Alternative Minimum Tax, which ensnared many affluent families:

I am lowering taxes far more than any other candidate. Any negotiated increase by Congress to my proposal would still be lower than current! (Donald Trump quoted in Luhby 2016).

Others also took issue with some of the assumptions of Bernie Sanders's economic program which he argued for during his campaign. Some economists called Sanders out for citing "extreme claims" that "exceed even the most grandiose predictions by the Republicans" (Krugman 2016b). Under Sanders, taxes—particularly on high earners—would have soared. He wanted to make public universities free, increase infrastructure spending, and expand Social Security (pensions). His most ambitious policy called for the government, rather than private insurers, to pay health-care bills. That would have cost $14 trillion over a decade, requiring new taxes on most workers worth 8.4 percent of their income (*Bernie Sanders' Economic Policy*, 2016).

Between Bernie Sanders and Donald Trump, both of whom lacked historical support from their respective parties and who possessed, at best, only a flimsy grasp of global issues, Americans regularly heard the same message of a nation under assault by Hillary Clinton. Their concurrent discourses were tailored to mesh with the affective states of each politician's "crowd of rage" base (Warren 2016), with relentless narrative blending variations of recurring and iconic images of a country and a people under siege. Common themes included America's pending demise, high taxes, excessive regulation, unpoliced borders, opposition to the Trans-Pacific Partnership, supporting Second Amendment gun rights, single-payer health care, low moral standards, unconstitutional government, inept foreign policy and a dwindling military, that the country was "going to hell," that Wall Street was corrupt and government "rigged," that "nothing less than a political revolution" would suffice, and that the American economy is failing (*Despite What Candidates Say* 2016; see also Zakaria 2016 and Dickinson 2015).

Rhetorical Parallels

Oratorically, what united them may be more significant than what divided them. While Bernie Sanders's style was that of a "finger-jabbing hoarse New Yorker remonstrating with a taxi driver who has just run over his foot" and Trump's is more "pomp and swagger," both are fundamentally united oratorically and have been described with terms such as "fervent incoherence" and descriptive phrases such as "your drunk uncle at a wedding." Each had "blindsided their respective political parties with "shouty populist" deliveries (Dickinson 2015).

Somewhat ironically but perhaps intentionally, and like Trump, what Sanders said was often "subtly at odds with his angle of attack." He was the anti-establishment politician making a case for the efficacy, or potential efficacy, of a political establishment; arguing that neither markets nor global climate are irreversible forces of nature: "The problems we face did not come down from the heavens. They are made. They are made by bad human decisions. And good human decisions can change them" (Sanders 2015a).

Sanders also emphasizes collective human agency in a way similar to Barack Obama—but where Obama peddled what Sarah Palin calls his "hopey-changey stuff" in an "historic high style," Bernie Sanders's rhetorical style mirrored Donald Trump's in that he did so "more like a man thumping the table in a bar" (Dickinson 2015). Trump and Sanders shared an angry tone and a raw, un-politician-like style that their affectively vulnerable albeit ideologically polarized supporters mutually embraced.

Donald Trump's rhetorical style was trademarked by an ability to reduce everything to black-and-white extremes of strong versus weak, greatest versus worst. He also played on simple, direct promises that "only he" could fill and dramatized problems that other politicians were too weak to manage. And he excelled at flouting "all the conventions of civilized discourse" when it came to any "others" he—and by default his base—deemed threatening. Accordingly, it was a benefit rather than a liability for Trump when he warned about Mexican rapists or spoke of killing Muslims with pigs-blood-tainted bullets. In so doing, Trump signaled his orphaned and authoritarian-leaning base that "political correctness" would "not hold him back from attacking the outgroups they fear" (Taub 2016).

Furthermore, although some "elitists" lampooned his "Apprentice-tv-star" persona, Donald Trump understood that politics for his supporters in particular was in part about being entertaining. As a result, Trump frequently "spoke from the heart" in unscripted so "not boring" talk which facilitated identification with his supporters and victory at the polls (quoted in *Top Takeaways from Nevada,* 2016). Finally, Egan (2016) reports that "professional truth-seekers have never seen anything like Trump" with regard to his ease with and skill at lying. Donald Trump has "perfected the outrageous untruth as a campaign tool," according to Florida A&M University professor Michael LaBossiere (quoted in Holan and Qiu 2015). The nonpartisan fact-checking website PolitiFact "awarded" his entire 2015 presidential campaign their "Lie of the Year" accolade. The organization rated 76 percent of Donald Trump's statements lies—57 percent false or mostly false, and another 19 percent "Pants on Fire" fabrications. Two percent of his assertions were rated true, and another six percent mostly true:

> It's the trope on Trump: He's authentic, a straight-talker, less scripted than traditional politicians. That's because Donald Trump doesn't let facts slow him down. Bending the truth or being unhampered by accuracy is a strategy he has followed for years (Holan and Qiu 2015).

POLICY PARALLELS

That Bernie Sanders and Donald Trump shared substantive common ground with regard to issues and intuitive understanding of their supporters spotlights why both held positions at odds with their respective party's platforms and also why both (but especially Trump, who held more positions at odds with the Republican platform) were perceived as such threats to their traditional party organizations (Dickinson 2015).

Saviors United Against Clinton

Both "outsider" candidates discursively created their own versions of "who" was responsible for their disenfranchised voters' anger, and each constantly invoked a "phantom solution" as easy and convenient remedies for the injustices their particular bases-segments felt were perpetrated by establishment politicians like Jeb Bush and Hillary Clinton. For example, Bernie Sanders blamed Wall Street bankers—among other "mainstream" bureaucrats and corporatists—for the troubles of his "orphaned" electorate and maintained "it is just too late for establishment politics and establishment economics" (quoted in Leibovich 2016). During a February 2016 press conference, he suggested that Clinton was beholding to "Wall Street and special interests":

> Here is the truth, and a very profound difference between Secretary Clinton and myself. Secretary Clinton has a number of super PACs, which today are raising very, very large sums of money from Wall Street and other powerful special interests (Sanders quoted in Foran 2016a).

Sanders talked up his own reliance on small-dollar fundraising and also implied that Clinton can't be trusted to stand with American workers by highlighting his record on trade policy. Trump framed immigrants, foreigners, and incompetent mainstream party leaders as the cause of his constituents' anger (Charen 2016). During a September 2016 rally, he insisted it was "sad" there was "no other way to fix our immigration system" except to "change our leadership in Washington":

> American lives have been stolen because our politicians have failed in their duty to secure our borders and enforce our laws like they have to be enforced. . . . Countless Americans who have died in recent years would be alive today if not for the open border policies of this administration and the administration that causes this horrible, horrible thought process, called Hillary Clinton (Trump 2016e).

Both Sanders and Trump agreed that American politics has been corrupted by "big money" which unfairly and heartlessly disadvantaged their constituents. Sanders demonstrated his independence from corporatism by funding his campaign from small donations; Trump demonstrated his freedom from the "big banks," certainly ironically, through relying on his enormous personal wealth to self-fund. Both also spoke directly to their combined base's fear of an America in decline; each challenged core elements of a failed bipartisan consensus that "exploded" in recession. In addition, both offered "muscular" economic policies which included indicting fair-trade policies which took away the jobs and wages of working-class Americans. Mainstream Republicans had recently joined with President Obama and the corporate lobby to pass "fast track trade authority" through Congress, while Hillary Clinton strategically took no position. In addition, on foreign policy, both Sanders and Trump opposed the invasion of Iraq while "mainstream" members of their parties supported it (Borosage 2015).

DIVIDED TOGETHER

In sum, although Bernie Sanders and Donald Trump were very different, their campaigns were not. Both were "anger candidates" (Cupp 2016) who carried "outsider" messages which targeted disenfranchised voters frustrated with the political establishment (Le Miere 2017). Fagen (2016) suggests a simplified synopsis of Sanders's and Trump's shared message: the system is rigged, the voters are "getting hosed," and I/we will make someone else pay. Trump "told it like it is" while Sanders was "authentic." Both bases "loved" their candidates' "outsiderism" and both sets of their mostly white and mostly male base were "mad as hell." Significantly, both Bernie Sanders and Donald Trump also intentionally created disruption and chaos in traditional American politics. To illustrate, many Americans were "jubilant" that, despite being waged by "an insane socialist demagogue and a foul-mouthed nationalist demagogue" their division-driven victories against "Wall Street-worshipping, establishment sellout" Hillary Clinton resulted in massive government "disruption" (Charen 2016 and Troy 2016).

Sanders vowed to participate in a "contested convention," despite being criticized by many in the Democratic establishment and also joined with Donald Trump in casting doubt on the legitimacy of the Democratic presidential election process. Sanders used Clinton's massive lead among Democratic superdelegates—elected officials and party officials who represent a small portion of the delegates needed to clinch the nomination—to illustrate how a "rigged system" was built to stymie insurgent candidacies. He reminded superdelegates that he polled better in hypothetical general-election matchups with Republican front-runner Donald Trump and reflected on the opposition that his campaign faced in the past year from many Democrats as he spoke at a May 2016 rally, observing that "we were taking on the entire Democratic Party establishment" and that it "looks like you're not intimidated by the establishment" (Sanders quoted in Tani 2016b).

At about this time, Donald Trump began directly quoting Sanders's statements about Hillary Clinton as the Republican candidate strategized for a presidential general-election matchup against Clinton, insisting that "Bernie Sanders has a message that's interesting" and that he could "reread some of his speeches and I can get some very good material" (quoted in Tani 2016a). This, despite maintaining that Trump and the Republican Party "don't need Bernie Sanders's critiques of the secretary" because they "have the resources to do all the opposition research they want on Secretary Clinton" (quoted in Tani 2016a), Sanders clearly had "no choice" over how the Republican used his words. Although Bernie Sanders "railed" publicly against Donald Trump's policies and rhetoric, Trump continued to co-opt Sanders's words by arguing the similarities of the two candidates' positions, particularly that Hillary Clinton was not fit to be president (Le Miere 2017). To illustrate, Trump repeated Sanders's assertion that "something is clearly lacking" in Hillary Clinton's judgment and insisted that Sanders "had said some things about her that are actually surprising" including "that essentially, she has no right to even be running and she's got bad judgment" (Trump quoted in Tani 2016a).

While Bernie Sanders ultimately endorsed Clinton and campaigned on her behalf (Le Miere 2017), his rhetoric, albeit perhaps unintentional, was likely a major factor in helping elevate Donald Trump to the American presidency. A portion of Sanders's "orphaned constituency" were so disappointed that Sanders did not receive "his" party's nomination, so angry with Hillary Clinton that she did and, as a result, so thoroughly disgusted with and divided from the Democratic Party that they voted for Donald Trump. A 2016 Cooperative Congressional Election Survey revealed that fully 12 percent of Bernie Sanders's supporters switched their allegiance to Donald Trump, providing large enough numbers on November 8, 2016, to sway the presidential election in favor of the Republican nominee. The impact of these votes was crucial because in each of the three states that ultimately swung the election for Trump—Michigan, Wisconsin and Pennsylvania—his margin of victory over Clinton was smaller than the number of Sanders base who voted for Trump. In other words, if the Sanders-Trump voters in those states had voted for Clinton, or even stayed home on Election Day, she would have won 46 more electoral votes, putting her at 278—enough to win (reported in Goddard 2017; see also Kurtzleben 2017). It is fairly certain the most crucial bond between Bernie Sanders and Donald Trump was not that they shared an upbringing in New York's outer boroughs or their joint "repugnance for trade deals" (Kazin 2016). Rather, it was that these two ideological adversaries were divided together against Hillary Clinton.

THREE

The "Outsider" Rhetorical Behavior of Bernie Sanders

The signature identifier of Bernie Sanders's populist rhetoric was the symbolism of his self-styled "outsider" identity. That identity allowed him to cast a wide net as a populist candidate dedicated to giving a voice to anyone in the political system, decent Americans in thrall to a clique of party elites and the wealthy who possess too much power and exert too much control. Sanders ran a remarkably effective campaign tapping the same anti-establishment fury Donald Trump stirred, albeit with a considerably different political outcome in mind save for winning. Hohmann (2016) suggests that Bernie Sanders, in order to assuage his ambition for a political revolution waged against mainstream politicians and corporatists, rhetorically "stoked" the anger of his base with messages which consistently warned of an American democracy in full retreat and calls for his base "to tear it all down," ostensibly in order to build "it" up again in his image. Sanders was aware of and spoke to that portion of the electorate who knew something was wrong, were clearly angry about it, and were looking for something or someone to blame. He told them who that was by:

> giving them a cabal of boogeyman bankers, corporations and allegedly bought politicians to bear the brunt of that resentment . . . through a fair degree of dishonesty . . . forming a mob of angry, misinformed people and then turning it on the likely Democratic nominee (Womack 2016).

MEDIATION STRATEGIES

As a result, just as Ralph Nader siphoned tens of thousands of votes on Election Day 2000 in Florida from Al Gore, possibly causing the deadlock and George W. Bush's victory, Bernie Sanders's similar "vampire effect" enfeebled Hillary Clinton. Troy (2016) suggests this dynamic followed a classic historical pattern. Sanders drew Clinton from the center toward the Democrats' extreme flank. That shift paralleled Jimmy Carter's leftward lurch when Ted Kennedy ran in 1980 and George H.W. Bush's right-wing swerve when Pat Buchanan rebelled in 1992. Each time, the front-runners felt forced to placate loyalists they should have been able to take for granted, while embracing extreme positions that haunted them during the general election campaign. 2016 replayed the insurgents' "vampire effect." Hillary Clinton expected to inherit the nomination without serious opponents. However, as an independent with no loyalty to a party, Sanders defaulted to themes of displacement and disempowerment, with Clinton at the epicenter of blame. When asked during the April 2016 primary debate if Hillary Clinton had the qualifications necessary to be president, Bernie Sanders admitted she had the "experience and the intelligence" to be a president but he did suggest Clinton seriously lacked qualifications in other areas:

> I question a judgment which voted for the war in Iraq—the worst foreign policy blunder in the history of this country, [Clinton] voted for virtually every disastrous trade agreement which cost us millions of decent-paying jobs. And I question her judgment about running super PACs which are collecting tens of millions of dollars from special interests, including $15 million from Wall Street. I don't believe that that is the kind of judgment we need to be the kind of president we need (Sanders 2016a).

Independent Democrat

That Bernie Sanders lacked any clear concept of party loyalty was not altogether surprising considering his history. When he entered the presidential race in October 2015 as a Democrat, he did so after serving sixteen years as Vermont's sole congressman before he was elected to the Senate in 2006, the longest-serving independent in congressional history (Rappeport 2015). At his April 2015 presidential announcement speech, Sanders insisted the United States had "more serious crises than any time since the Great Depression of the 1930s" and that there were "enormous issues" facing the country. He also immediately identified himself as an "outsider" candidate with little allegiance to the status quo in several different ways:

> You are looking at a guy indisputably, who has the most unusual political history of anybody in the United States Congress. It's not only that

I am the longest serving independent in the history of the United States Congress, I have run for statewide office and I got one percent of the vote. I don't know if I should be proud of that, but in my last election, I got 71 percent of the vote. The point is, that's not the right question. The question is, if you raise the issues that are on the hearts and minds of the American people, if you try to put a movement together that says, we have got to stand together as a people and say that, this capitol, this beautiful capitol, our country belonged to all of us, and not the billionaire class, that is not raising an issue. That is winning elections. That is where the American people are (Sanders 2015a).

Others have suggested that Sanders's identification as a Democrat was pragmatic and more about labels than media coverage. He simply understood that he could never occupy the White House as an independent. As such, he campaigned as a faux Democrat "trashing other Democrats" to the extent that the bulk of his negative messaging was not about the GOP but about the Democratic Party and "its most likely nominee" (Alperstein 2016). During a March 2015 town hall meeting, Sanders was asked by an Ohio voter why he chose to run as a Democrat, despite having served for years as an independent. He explained that a candidate would have to be "a billionaire" to run as an independent, so:

We did have to make that decision: do you run as an independent? Do you run within the Democratic Party? We concluded—and I think it was absolutely the right decision—that . . . in terms of media coverage, you had to run within the Democratic Party" (Sanders quoted in Bump 2016b).

The "Bernie Base"

It is likely that Sanders ran as a Democrat because he recognized that "blazing his own trail through the political wilderness didn't make sense." The Democratic Party—with which he has caucused for years—had "already done that hard work." Because of that work, he could inhabit the Democratic campaign infrastructure which was already in place and within which he constructed his own outsider campaign. His competitive "edge" then became sharper as it was honed by an Internet-organized and social media-savvy "Bernie-bot" base. That base, in turn, received an enormous boost (as did his candidacy, media presence, and ethos) because so many of his voters were actually independents and not Democrats. Alperstein (2016) describes an adjacent group of Bernie Sanders's supporters, the "BernieBros," usually white men, who primarily trolled women who "dared" question their candidate or commented in a pro-Hillary way on social media sites. As such, Bump's assessment of Democratic party elders' concerns that Bernie Sanders really did not actually care or even need the party, was that those concerns were "mostly true" (2016b).

To further illustrate Sanders's "I'm running for president as a Democrat but I am really an independent" candidacy, while never saying "lock her up," as the primary election moved into the general, Sanders made little attempt to "disentangle" Hillary Clinton from the DNC's "rigging." In addition, his surrogates and supporters constantly complained with little challenge from their candidate that the party was a "monolith" which forced Clinton's nomination "against the will of the people." Also, when asked by a reporter during the primaries if he would describe Clinton as the "lesser of two evils" when compared to Trump, Sanders implied that while he "wouldn't describe" her in those specific words, nevertheless "that's what the American people are saying." Nor did he attempt to correct his base of "Bernie or Busters" when they insisted: "If we don't get Bernie, we're not just going to automatically vote for the demon" or actress Susan Sarandon when she insisted that Hillary Clinton was "more dangerous" than Donald Trump (Daou 2016b).

Sanders was often at the helm of his campaign's rage against Hillary Clinton and the Democratic Party, to the extent that the overall message, direction, and strategy of the campaign was his. To illustrate, he made the choice to go after Democratic National Committee chair Debbie Wasserman Schultz after his wife Jane Sanders read Sanders a transcript of Schultz's televised criticism of her husband (Dovere and Debenedetti 2016). He also asserted "I don't think you are qualified" in response to Clinton's position on a free-trade agreement with which he disagreed, a strategy against which some aides had argued out of concern that such a statement might erase any hope for Sanders of winning in New York and a last chance of turning a losing primary run around (Sanders quoted in Engel 2016).

Super Delegate Bob Mulholland wrote directly to Sanders in response to the many complaints from other unbound delegates to the National Convention in Philadelphia who had received harassing emails, Facebook postings, and phone calls "demanding we support you":

> We would expect this type of bullying tactics from Trump supporters. Roger Stone threatened on April 5th—he will send angry Trump supporters to the hotel rooms (Cleveland) of any delegates who betray Donald. Do you have a similar plan? Society has been trying to deal with high school bullies and the same rule should apply to your campaign and your supporters (2016).

While noting that Hillary Clinton might have made "a few more moves" to ease the tension caused by the fight over delegates and resulting "ugly behavior," Cooper (2016a) suggests Sanders's failures to bring about reconciliation were "far worse." Nevada political journalist Jon Ralston reports that, as the Nevada Democratic Convention shut down, Sanders's delegates "hurled ugly epithets" at Clinton surrogate Barbara Boxer, and used a sign to block her from being shown on big screens. They also "screamed vulgarities" at state Chairwoman Roberta Lange, who later received death threats after Sanders's followers posted her cell phone number and home address online and threw chairs at the stage as they tried to control a convention they had lost. The next day, members of Sanders's base protested at the state Democratic Party headquarters and wrote phrases including "murdered democracy" and "you are scum" on outside walls and sidewalks (cited in Cooper 2016a).

Sanders "had a chance to strongly denounce what happened" the next day but "blew it" despite assuring reporters he would make a "strong statement" about what happened in Nevada. Instead, his campaign offered a generic statement which first reiterated their candidates' grievance with the Democratic National Committee and then revisited what they believed to be unfair treatment Sanders received from the DNC. An "our campaign of course believes in nonviolent change" assertion followed. This was not a particularly strategic rhetorical choice if Sanders was actually interested in persuading his supporters to "calm down":

> You need to put the condemnation on top instead of defiantly proclaiming your victimhood. You're not Mississippi civil rights legend Fannie Lou Hamer trying to get seated at the Democratic convention in 1964 (Cooper 2016a; see also Daou 2016a).

Alperstein (2016) maintains that Bernie Sanders failed to "set an example at the top" in that he failed to proactively and consistently call out members of his base who used "loaded gendered language" or booed Hillary Clinton openly at rallies while at the same time actively encourage those same supporters to view the Democratic front-runner as "untrustworthy, power-driven and corrupt."

Splintering the Party

Krugman (2016c) believes that some of Sanders's ideas including his political theory of change and waving away of limits "seems utterly unrealistic." His political discourse consisted primarily of relentless and laser-targeted appeals to a young, generally well-educated, and primarily white portion of disenfranchised American voters. This rhetoric was successful to such an extent that it "splintered and ultimately sabotaged the Democratic party" not because Sanders chose to run against Clinton, but because of how he ran against her" (Bordo 2017). An outcome of this strategy was that his "orphaned" and partisan base considered "Clintonian centrism not liberal enough, not minority-sensitive enough, not pure enough" to such an extent that Sanders became the only person they "felt truly deserved their votes" (Troy 2016; Bordo 2017). A second and more significant result was the election of Donald Trump, "a president-elect hostile to liberalism, unafraid of demonizing minorities and epitomizing a killer instinct that makes Clintonian triangulation look naïve" (Troy 2016).

POLITICAL REVOLUTION

Bernie Sanders made a case for a political revolution which challenged and transformed corrupted politics enacted through a popular movement situated within progressive democratic socialism. Sanders spoke to what he perceived as discontent with the "abuses and excesses of capitalism as well as corporate control of politics." His primary target was entrenched corporate interests and big money that constantly and unfairly ruled against his base (Borosage 2015). Sanders did so, in part, by trying to turn the focus of the Democratic Party away from a combination of "crony capitalism" and identity politics toward a focus on the effect economic change has had on the "security and dignified autonomy of ordinary Americans" by appealing to a nostalgia of an imagined past which resonated with his disaffected segment of the public. To illustrate, Sanders challenged his disenfranchised base to mobilize and engage in order to return "our" democracy to them, vowing that "it is time to break these too-big-to-fail banks" so they "can never again destroy the jobs, homes, and life savings of the American people" (Sanders quoted in Mahbubani 2016).

White and Privileged

In addition, Sanders offered a specific agenda to his disillusioned base, essentially a revival and updating of the Democrats' last winning agenda: an updated version of an outdated concept that appealed to a public which was primarily elite, white, college-educated, and "FDR-nostaglic." While a version of the Roosevelt agenda was a popular theme in many statehouses it was nonetheless generally off the radar for the cultural, gender, and minority rights activists who made up the party's core activist base. Sanders wanted an updated New Deal but, rather than calling for a genuine revolution, he was basically demanding the Democratic party return to a principle it "used to champion" and possibly still believed in but was in fact no longer at the top of the agenda for mainstream and activist Democrats (J. J. Goldberg 2015; see also Geiger 2016).

Like Trump, Sanders tended to ignore the issue of racism, albeit to a different degree and no doubt for different reasons. Achen and Bartels (2016) contend that rather than being concentrated among "liberal ideologues," Sanders shared another similarity with Trump in that his support consisted mostly of disaffected white men. Regardless, Marche (2016) suggests that a fundamental difference between the two campaigns with regard to race was that "the Sanders crowd" had more money than Trump's base. Therefore, Sanders could attempt to include "all races" in his vision of social democracy because "rich white people" could "afford to think about socialism" while Trump's base of "the poor" could "only afford anger."

Williams (2017) identifies "race" as the single issue "which emerged as the Achilles' heel of Sanders's remarkable bid for the presidency." Marche (2016) contends that the same specter of angry white men, driven by the "same sense of longing for a country that has been taken away," haunted Bernie Sanders's rallies. Rosario (2016) argues that criticizing black voters for not supporting Sanders when he chose deliberately to ignore them is problematic. Despite having substantial funds to invest in inner city organizing, Bernie Sanders chose, instead, to invest in white-majority regions "at the expense of the Deep South and urban North." This was likely not accidental as Sanders prioritized issues such as economic justice and checking the power of the wealthy over racial equality which he believed was contingent on economic equality. Another way to think about the strategy of the Sanders campaign with regard to race is that it was based on the premise that if only progressives were to make a clear enough case about the evils of inequality among individuals, they could win over the whole working class, regardless of race (Mahbubani 2016 and Krugman 2016d; see also J. J. Goldberg 2015).

The Democratic candidate's insistence on a relentless condemnation of "millionaires and billionaires," along with his focus on sweeping change, and revolution in the form of a progressive agenda as well as a stalwart rejection of compromise, all "litmus tests few viable black candidates could pass," for the most part kept African Americans away from Sanders's campaign. These priorities were foregrounded in Sanders's 2015 presidential announcement speech:

> This country today in my view, has more serious crises than any time since the Great Depression of the 1930s. . . . My kid can't afford to go to college, and I'm having a hard time affording health care. What happened, while at exactly the same time, 99 percent of the income being generated in this country is going to the top 1 percent? . . . My conclusion is that that type of economics is not only immoral, is wrong, it is unsustainable. It can't continue. . . . The major issue is how do we create an economy that works for all of our people rather than a small number of billionaires, and the second issue, directly related, is the fact that as a result of the disastrous Supreme Court decision on Citizens United, we now have a political situation where billionaires are literally able to buy themselves elections and candidates. . . . . In my state of Vermont, and throughout this country, young people, bright, young, able kids, cannot afford to go to college and are leaving school deeply in debt. In Germany, countries around the world, they understand that you tap the intellectual capabilities of young people, and you make college tuition in public colleges and universities free. That is my view as well. . . . I believe that in a democracy, what elections are about are

serious debates about serious issues, not political gossip, not making campaign soap operas. This is not the Red Sox versus the Yankees. This is the debate over major issues facing the American people (quoted in Wood 2015).

"Channeling Hugo Chavez," Sanders's promises included lifting the minimum wage, providing free college education for all, and delivering universal health care with only a small tax required of the middle class. All would pay, including bloated corporations, mainstream politicians, and self-serving bureaucrats as retribution for oppressing those who were now Bernie Sanders's base:

The greed, the recklessness, and the illegal behavior drove our econo-my to its knees. The American people bailed out Wall Street, now it's Wall Street's time to help the middle class (Sanders quoted in Charen 2016).

Ball (2016) believes that a primary reason Bernie Sanders did not pay much attention to the "issue of race" during his campaign was that it "simply" was not an issue about which he was "passionate" in the way he was "passionate about economic injustice." His career in public life had been "laser focused on checking the power of the wealthy above all else" which resulted in Sanders's belief that "focusing on racial issues first" was "merely treating the symptom, not the disease." In Goldberg's (2015) view, that Bernie Sanders was "after bigger fish" than minority rights, left him with a "radioactive but inescapable" reality that:

as long as Democrats insist on him being seen primarily as the voice of minorities, the majority will continue to shop elsewhere. And that when that happens, the Republicans win and the minorities end up with nothing.

Outcome: A Pivot?

Bernie Sanders's most obvious discursive strategy after Clinton and Trump had won their respective party's nominations was to continue to attack Trump. However, rather than overtly campaign for Clinton as "his party's" candidate, Sanders rhetorically backgrounded the Democratic nominee in favor of continuing to advance, at fundamentally every op-portunity, his own political agenda of "social revolution." Weeks after Clinton had officially secured the majority of pledged delegates, and still providing no endorsement of her candidacy, Sanders was still delivering his stump speeches, many broadcasted through national media, insisting his political revolution was just beginning (Bordo 2017). In this sense, much as Trump continued to appeal most often to his partisan and disaf-fected base, so Sanders continued to do the same for his base. Even when no longer running for the presidency, he used his supporters as a sort of bargaining currency to advance his agenda with the party. Shortly after it became clear that Hillary Clinton was the Democratic nominee, Sanders spoke at a rally in his home state of Vermont and clarified that electing Hillary Clinton as the next president was not the most important post-primary goal:

> The major political task that we face in the next five months is to make certain that Donald Trump is defeated [but] defeating Donald Trump cannot be our only goal. We must continue our grassroots efforts to create the America that we know we can become. And we must take that energy into the Democratic National Convention on July 25 in Philadelphia where we will have more than 1,900 delegates (Sanders 2016b).

Sanders reminded his supporters that "this campaign has never been about any single candidate" but rather "it is always about transforming America" and spoke about what was most important in guaranteeing that transformation in the future. He did so by demanding that his base made sure the "revolution continued," implying that this might occur possibly without Clinton as president unless she could "toe the line" of his/their demands, agenda, and dreams. These demands included revising a "corrupt" campaign finance system, ending the "grotesque" wealth of the "people at the top," and creating an economy that "works for all of us, not just the 1 percent." Furthermore it was about "ending the disgrace of native Americans" who have "a life expectancy lower than many third-world countries." It was also about addressing the "incredible despair" in the country, the result of chronic unemployment, suicide, and drugs such that "millions of Americans are now dying, in an ahistorical way, at a younger age than their parents"; living in a country with one of the highest levels of childhood poverty "on earth" and "having public school systems in inner cities that are totally failing our children—where kids now stand a greater chance of ending up in jail than ending up with a college degree" (Sanders 2016b).

A Perpetual Candidate

After once again reminding his supporters that "this election" was not "just" about defeating Donald Trump and that "it is no secret that Secretary Clinton and I have strong disagreements on some very important issues," Sanders carefully detailed some of those same issues. In so doing, he also again employed the rhetoric of divisiveness and partisanship with which he successfully grew his base but, significantly at this point in time, which also functioned at a critical time for the Democrats, to divide these young, disaffected voters from their own party. Sanders spoke of raising the federal minimum wage to create jobs and rebuild a "crumbling infrastructure." He also warned of a president who ignored the gross income inequality and gave "billions of dollars in tax breaks" to the wealthy, called for the defeat of the Trans-Pacific Partnership, demanded resistance in attempts to limit Social Security, and insisted that benefits be expanded for seniors and veterans. Other themes included holding Wall Street accountable of its greed and illegal activity, passing "modern-day" Glass-Steagall legislation, and demolishing the nation's financial institutions who "not only remain too big to fail" but who also block the competition required in a robust and healthy financial system. In addition, Sanders demanded tuition-free universities as well as major reductions in student debt (Sanders 2016b).

He then urged supporters to continue accessing the "Bernie.com" website for additional post-campaign/pro-"Bernie revolution" strategy suggestions and concluded by explaining the vital role "orphaned" supporters played in transforming the Democratic party and getting rid of its mainstream leaders, possibly even Clinton if she did not demonstrate allegiance to their goals:

> But the political revolution means much more than fighting for our ideals at the Democratic National Convention and defeating Donald Trump. . . . It means that we can no longer ignore the fact that, sadly, the current Democratic Party leadership has turned its back on dozens of states in this country and has allowed right-wing politicians to win elections in some states with virtually no opposition—including some of the poorest states in America. . . . Most importantly, the Democratic Party needs leadership which is prepared to open its doors and welcome into its ranks working people and young people. . . . Let me conclude by once again thanking everyone who has helped in this campaign in one way or another. We have begun the long and arduous process of transforming America, a fight that will continue tomorrow, next week, next year and into the future (Sanders 2016b).

Finally, he hoped that history would remember a successful insurgency of Bernie Sanders rather than a failed presidency of Hillary Rodham Clinton:

> My hope is that when future historians look back and describe how our country moved forward into reversing the drift toward oligarchy, and created a government which represents all the people and not just the few, they will note that, to a significant degree, that effort began with the political revolution of 2016 (Sanders 2016b).

On the first day of the Democratic National Convention, while ultimately vowing to "stand with her" as the nominee, Sanders "walked out on stage to rapturous applause from supporters who, earlier in the day, had made their displeasure with the results of the 14-month contest very clear" to essentially deliver the same message he had two weeks before in New Hampshire when he first endorsed Clinton (for a text-by-text comparison see Bump 2016e). If no longer a viable candidate, Sanders made it clear that he nonetheless still held the power and allegiance of his progressive but "orphaned" base. Furthermore, he would hold Clinton and the Democratic party accountable to that base and their demands. While "proud to stand with her today," Sanders reminded and tacitly warned that:

> It is no secret that Hillary Clinton and I disagree on a number of issues. That's what this campaign has been about. That's what democracy is about. But I am happy to tell you that at the Democratic Platform Committee which ended Sunday night in Orlando, there was a significant coming together between the two campaigns and we produced, by far, the most progressive platform in the history of the Democratic Party. Our job now is to see that platform implemented by a Democratic Senate, a Democratic House and a Hillary Clinton presidency—and I am going to do everything I can to make that happen. (Sanders 2016c).

By the Philadelphia convention, Sanders was confident enough to detail some of the platform additions he had won for his ten million strong "orphaned" Democrats:

> Among many other strong provisions, the Democratic Party now calls for breaking up the major financial institutions on Wall Street and the passage of a 21st Century Glass-Steagall Act. It also calls for strong opposition to job-killing free trade agreements like the Trans-Pacific Partnership (Sanders 2016d).

Some have suggested that, post-convention, it became obvious Bernie Sanders was not then nor had he ever been loyal to the Democratic party. Rather, he had utilized party resources to "launch a full-frontal attack" to tear down the "Democratic Party Establishment" through attacks on the character, credibility, and integrity of Hillary Clinton as well as of the party and its members. One Democrat observed that Sanders created a toxic "demonizing narrative" among his followers that "handed Donald Trump numerous soundbites" (Lightner 2016).

By June 2016 while campaign aides dismissed the idea their candidate could be damaging the party and hurting Clinton, they did acknowledge that Bernie Sanders was "at the heart of the rage against Hillary Clinton" (Dovere and Debenedetti 2016). Troy (2016) maintains that by Election Day, Sanders had earned the 2016 "Ralph Nader Award" for the "Leftist Most Responsible for Helping Republicans Win the Presidency" (see also Tani 2016a; Tani 2016b). Sanders's strategic and incessant attacks against Clinton, combined with Trump's "clever exploitation" of voters' frustrations, contributed to Clinton's loss. By rhetorically exploiting and energizing his base with the same strategies he had used during the primaries, Sanders created an "insurgency" within the Democratic party. And it was this insurgency which pushed Clinton so "far to the left" as she attempted to "woo" Sanders's constituency, that she was prevented from "an effective re-centering in the fall." The result was the failure of Hillary Rodham Clinton to unify the nation and the loss of the presidency.

FOUR

The "Outsider" Rhetorical Behavior of Donald Trump

The celebrity status of Donald Trump was not the only factor that catapulted him to the top of the Republican party, despite his lack of political experience. In Madden's (2015) view, the experience deficit made voters more willing to accept him as a legitimate candidate for the presidency in part because a substantial portion of the American public was already disenchanted by the political process and, more specifically, politicians before his ascension. It also afforded him a political persona generally more flexible than that of a professional politician, which meant he could take his campaign in generally any direction he wished (*Time to Fire Trump* 2016). Trump's base often cited their attraction to him because "he tells it like it is" (Fagen 2016).

A constant in Donald Trump's view of Donald Trump which he presented to his base was that America only needs a "great leader" (himself) to rid the country of bad leaders, make America great again and, in so doing, make life for his "orphaned" audience great again as well:

> Our country needs a truly great leader, and we need a truly great leader now. We need a leader that wrote "The Art of the Deal." We need a leader that can bring back our jobs, can bring back our manufacturing, can bring back our military.... And we also need a cheerleader. We need someone who can take the brand of the United States and make it great again. We need—we need somebody—we need somebody that literally will take this country and make it great again. We can do that (quoted in Borosage 2015).

University of Houston researcher Jennifer Wingard suggests a key shift in American political rhetoric over the past several election cycles has been to a focus on spectacle rather than reasoned debate. Accordingly, it was not Donald Trump's position on any particular political issue that won him the presidency but that he was and remains a "veritable cash cow" for advertisers, and so was/is guaranteed to remain at the top of each news cycle (quoted in Ross 2015). In the words of Roger Stone, former political advisor to Donald Trump:

> I am so proud of Donald Trump . . . and I think he's on his way to the nomination and on his way to the White House. . . . Elitists like to make fun of Trump because he was a reality TV star. But Trump understands that politics is about being entertaining. The worst thing you can do in politics other than being wrong is to be boring. . . . Trump is unscripted. He's not talking from a speech written by someone else. He's not making his speech based on polling or focus groups, or words put in his mouth. He speaks from the heart. And that's what voters are identifying with. That's exactly why he is doing so well. There's nothing phony about Donald Trump. He's the real deal. . . . What I'm saying is that the mass coverage of our politics and the fact that voters find cold policy boring means that you have to make your positions and your standing interesting to the voters. This probably wasn't true before the invention of television, when we operated through hand bills and newspapers. But it's just a reality of how we communicate today (*Top Takeaways from Nevada,* 2016).

MEDIATION STRATEGIES

Poniewozik (2017) describes Donald Trump as "all volatile rage" and his 2016 campaign as "ugly, intense and personal," as he engaged Clinton through "an appeal to tribe and vitriol that simply wasn't equal on both sides." Described by Dovere (2017) as a man "who ran one of the most divisive campaigns in one of the most divisive elections in history," Donald Trump was skilled at focusing attention on foregrounding America as a country which wins while others lose. He countered President Obama's claim to be a citizen of the world, and alleged that the president is not sufficiently attuned to what's best for America. Peter Lawler, a professor of government at Berry College, contends that a sign of the "decaying quality in the basic classiness of American political rhetoric" was the use of expletives (curse words) in speeches, particularly for Donald Trump:

> His Jacksonian brand is to show he can say anything—things that are not only politically incorrect but offenses against common decency—and get away with it" (cited in Ross 2015).

Because each anecdotal "Trumpism" seemed less shocking than the one before, there was a danger of becoming desensitized to his sensationalized discourse and assertions which included labeling Mexicans crossing the border as "rapists"; enthusiastic endorsement of torture; hinting that Antonin Scalia, a Supreme Court justice, was murdered; proposing banning all Muslims from the United States; advocating killing the families of terrorists and volunteered he would like to "punch a protestor in the face." He also repeated, approvingly, a "damaging fiction" that a century ago American soldiers in the Philippines dipped their ammunition in pigs' blood before executing Muslim rebels. Trump's outsider mediation strategies, which provoked one journalist to assert that "almost the only policy Mr. Trump clearly subscribes to is a fantasy" included the construction of a wall along the southern border, paid for by Mexico:

> What would he do if faced with a crisis in the South China Sea, a terrorist attack in America or another financial meltdown? Nobody has any idea. Mr. Trump may be well suited to campaigning in primaries, where voters bear little resemblance to the country as a whole, but it is difficult to imagine any candidate less suited to the consequence of winning a general election, namely governing (*Time to Fire Trump,* 2016).

Exploitation of Clinton

Nevius (2016) contends Donald Trump's candidacy upended the traditional political narrative in the United States in ways that "will be dissected for years." While his celebrity, outsider status and "Twitter outbursts" initially separated him, what primarily set him apart from other candidates was that he appeared to be "completely immune to one of the most damaging accusations in politics: the "flip-flop" (Nevius 2016). In Troy's (2016) view, having catered to the millennial and minority sensibility in the spring, Hillary Clinton missed the mainstream, failing to recalibrate for the fall. This misread was most apparent in her neglect of her greatest political ally, Bill Clinton, and his legacy. In the 1990s, President Clinton led from the center, forging a "Third Way" progressivism more balanced than the big-government, special interest group-oriented liberalism which Ronald Reagan and George H.W. Bush handily defeated in the 1980s. In 2016, pressed by the Sanders campaign, intimidated by Black Lives Matter, "even" Bill Clinton backpedaled, apologizing for fighting crime and his centrist legacy. With no one explaining how bad crime was in the 1990s, how dysfunctional the welfare system was, how two-thirds of blacks supported both initiatives, Hillary Clinton's legislation seemed draconian. In this way, she became a "doughnut candidate, sprinkling sweets to particular groups but lacking any core." That distortion made her the perfect foil for Donald Trump's "mob democracy" appeals (Troy 2016; see also Williamson 2016).

The media has made the individual persona or narrative, regardless of truth, endlessly reproducible through the electronic channels of Twitter and Facebook. Trump clearly recognized this. His stint on "The Apprentice" proved that a "Lifestyles of the Rich and Famous" manner was ultimately adaptable to a "twenty-first century cultural tenor." Trump relied primarily on his rally-rhetoric and social media presence to exploit real fears already present in his base, which he combined with "virtually any unmoored fact" to mobilize those fears:

> He has a bottomless bank account to back it up. Add in a white, increasingly old middle class, palpably anxious about whether their days are numbered that can seal themselves in a media bubble echo chamber . . . and you've gone a long way toward explaining what's underneath Trump's poll numbers—and what makes him somewhat exceptional (Billet 2016).

With an eighteen-month campaign for president and a continual news cycle, there was a constant need for headlines for which Donald Trump, a reality-show star with extensive experience in self-promotion, was "uniquely positioned to give the media the headlines . . . to fill the weeks between debates and months before real votes are cast" (S. Shapiro 2015). Donald Trump's digital campaign manager recalls that he reweighted their model after he "had a hunch" from reading Breitbart, Reddit, Facebook, and other "nontraditional" news sources that angry and disaffected segments of the electorate were being missed by traditional pollsters and mainstream media (cited in Halpern 2017). It was this marginalized group which became Trump's base and pushed him to electoral victory over Hillary Clinton as "a genuine impresario of the mob." In this way, Trump became "an instrument of the crowd" able to "feel its resentment, its impatience, its distrust." He "returned them all in slogans and epithets" which validated the "crowd's malice by speaking out loud things people are not sure they have a right to say" (Traub 2016).

Trump's celebrity facilitated an awareness that politics was about spectacle and being entertaining which enabled the development of a rhetorical style which resonated successfully with his base.

Appeals to White Fear and Anger

Wehner (2016) believes that Donald Trump's conservatism was not that of William F. Buckley, Jr., or Ronald Regan or Jack Kemp but, instead, was a "blood-and-soil conservatism" aimed at alienated white voters who believed they had lost the country they once knew. After Trump was widely condemned for retweeting a graphic of homicide data delineated by race, FactCheck.org found that "almost every figure in the graphic is wrong." His response on the Bill O'Reilly Show was:

> Bill, I didn't tweet, I retweeted somebody that was supposedly an expert, and it was also a radio show . . . am I gonna check every statistic? . . . All it was is a retweet. And it wasn't from me. It came out of a radio show, and other places. . . . This was a retweet. And it comes from sources that are very credible, what can I tell you? (quoted in Mercieca 2016).

And when Gawker tricked Trump into retweeting a quote from Benito Mussolini, his response was "what difference does it make whether it's Mussolini or somebody else? It's certainly a very interesting quote" (quoted in Mercieca 2016). Wallis (2016) suggests Trump appealed to this base of generally older, white, male evangelicals through blatant racist rhetoric, particularly framing white men as "outsider" victims of a "too" racially diverse country:

> He is the white candidate, the white nationalist champion, the leader who promises to block, obstruct, deny, or at least delay the . . . America that is emerging. It is time to admit that the word "white" is wiping out the word "evangelical" . . . Trump, the "birther," has long led a racially motivated campaign questioning the citizenship of the first black president. All the "outsider" analysis of Trump's success that fails to use the word race misses this core of his campaign (Wallis 2016; see also Wendling 2016, and Tyson and Manium 2016).

Trump's campaign tapped into a "vein of nativism" in a way that "previous nominees had left well alone." For example, after introducing Mike Pence as his running mate, Trump said "We are the law and order candidates" and the Republican Party was the "law-and-order party." It has been suggested the phrase was a stand-in for "Americanism," a code for "law-abiding" and "white" (Trump quoted in Jerde 2016; see also *Americanism, a Presidential Gambit,* 2016). Early in the presidential campaign, Waldman (2015) stated that after decades of "rhetorical evolution from Republicans on matters of race" Donald Trump was "now running the most plainly, explicitly, straightforwardly racist campaign since at least George Wallace's third-party run in 1968, and maybe even Strom Thurmond's in 1948" (see also R. Jones 2016; Pillar 2016 and Kristof 2016). To illustrate, it has been suggested that Trump clearly evidenced racism when he refused to "immediately and unequivocally denounce and disavow the former Ku Klux Klan grand wizard David Duke and enacted a campaign which provided a "refuge for" and gave "voice to, white fear and anger over the inevitable changing demography of the country, the erosion of the center and the rewarding of whiteness as a commodity" (Blow 2016a). And in May 2016, Donald Trump implied that Gonzalo Curiel, an American citizen born in Indiana, and the federal judge presiding over a class action against the for-profit Trump University, could not fairly hear the case because of his Mexican heritage:

> He's a Mexican. We're building a wall between here and Mexico. The answer is, he is giving us very unfair rulings—rulings that people can't even believe (Trump quoted in Terkel 2016a).

Since the American campaign for civil rights in the 1960s, virtually all presidential campaigns have included accusations that candidates appealed to antidemocratic and racist sentiments through the use of code words. This strategy was made "explicit" as early as 1981, when the

Republican strategist Lee Atwater explained in a radio interview that politicians, who by around 1968 could no longer use the word "nigger" to assault people of color, resorted to abstracting the issue by talking about "forced busing," "states' rights" and "cutting taxes" (quoted in Stanley 2015). A prototypic "violation" of this sort occurred in 2012, when Republican nominee Mitt Romney faced criticism for his campaign claim that President Obama wanted to eliminate work requirements from welfare (cited in Stanley 2015). However, the 2016 race has been different, as evidenced by Donald Trump's "now infamous" and obviously racist statement made during the speech in which he announced his candidacy:

> When Mexico sends its people, they're not sending their best. They're not sending you. They're sending people that have lots of problems, and they're bringing those problems with us. They're bringing drugs. They're bringing crime. They're rapists. And some, I assume, are good people (Trump 2015).

Trump's statement appeared to have been rewarded:

> at least [as indicated] in [his] immediate improvements in poll standings [which] confronts defenders of the American political system [with the realization] that there once was [and no longer is] a facade of equal respect that required political strategists to use code words to avoid accusations of violating it (Stanley 2015).

Trump seemed to prosper by inciting hatred and violence with such confidence that it appeared the Republican was clearly not stymied by any second guessing about or lack of confidence in his own opinions. Waldman (2016) argues Trump's racism was about both "rhetoric and substance." For example, a stylistic element was revealed in the way Trump gave people permission during his campaign to let their ugliest beliefs out for display, with no fear of being silenced by "political correctness." There were also consequences to such discourse. When he told voters to hate and fear others who did not look like them, he also implored them to action. At a rally, Trump promised "we are going to be so tough, we are going to be so smart and so vigilant and we're going to get it so that people turn in people when they know there's something going on," complaining that too many people were worried about being accused of racial profiling to turn in their neighbors (Trump quoted in Waldman 2016). Republican strategist and media consultant Rick Wilson called out his party's support of Donald Trump's racism and what that brought to the table, arguing that while there was "a quick way to stop this without too much fuss" the party would not "for fear of offending" Trump:

> [And] he won't, for fear of offending his base. Under his "Taco Salad! I love the Jews! Look at my African-American!" bluster, he's a crafty bastard who understands white resentment politics. They're a feature,

not a bug. They're not part of his play; they're his only play (Wilson quoted in S. Jones 2016).

Appeals to Misogyny and Nationalism

Stuckey (2016) asserts Donald Trump's base was constructed of whites who believed that their place in the national order was threatened and shrinking. He was a major party candidate who "brought out the latent Republican Party 'dog whistle' politics [and] who implied that Megyn Kelly's 'tough' questions were evidence of her menstrual cycle; [and] who argued that women who obtain abortions should be punished, and perhaps even imprisoned." Trump has been called out for a misogynistic framing of women, which was "even beyond the troubling racial realities of his candidacy." "This is a man who has called various women 'disgusting,' 'a slob,' 'grotesque,' 'a dog.' And he says that he cherishes women" (Trump quoted in Blow 2016a). On April 25, 2016, the day before the Pennsylvania primaries, Trump appeared on *Fox and Friends*, and introduced the term "Crooked Hillary" (with his evidence for the term being "because she's crooked"). In the same interview he also declared of Clinton that "the only thing she's got is the woman card" (Bordo 2017).

RHETORICAL ASSASSINATION OF CLINTON

Donald Trump created a polarizing rhetoric which played to and reinforced his outsider ethos with which he framed Hillary Clinton as a dysfunctional and abusive mainstream political animal. Over 40 percent of the discourse with which he exclusively targeted Clinton after the primaries included ad hominem attacks (Natale 2016). Other strategies included apocalyptic and misogynistic framing; the use of vague and loaded terms; pandering; scapegoating; demonizing, and appeals to uber-nationalism, all components of character assassination discourse. During an August 2016 speech in New York City, Donald Trump delivered a full throttle rhetorical assault against the Democratic frontrunner. He detailed problems facing his supporters including "crumbling roads" and "factories moving overseas to Mexico" noting all could be fixed "but not by Hillary Clinton—only me." Trump then elaborated, accusing Clinton of being "a world class liar" and a thief who "let China steal hundreds of billions of dollars" from which she "gets rich making you poor." Furthermore, she "sold out our workers, and our country, for Beijing" and would continue to "ship millions more of our jobs overseas." He continued by insisting Clinton had:

> betrayed the American worker on trade at every single stage of her career [and] cost America thousands of lives and trillions of dollars [to the extent that]no Secretary of State has been more wrong, more often,

and in more places than Hillary Clinton. . . . Her decisions spread
death, destruction and terrorism everywhere she touched. Among the
victims is our late Ambassador, Chris Stevens . . . left helpless to die as
Hillary Clinton soundly slept in her bed. She started the war that put
him in Libya, denied him the security he asked for, then left him there
to die. To cover her tracks, Hillary lied (Trump 2016b).

In order to prove Clinton's "tryout for the presidency" had resulted in
"one deadly foreign policy disaster after another" Trump discursively led
his base through a litany of Clinton's faults and weaknesses. She had
destabilized the "entire Middle East," given Egypt to radical Muslims,
handed Libya to the "ISIS barbarians," and was the reason "ISIS threatens us today." Clinton rushed the United States "off to war in Libya,"
further evidence that she "lacks the temperament, the judgment and the
competence to lead." The "most terrifying thing about" her was a foreign
policy which refused to acknowledge the "threat posed by radical Islam":

> Under her plan, we would admit hundreds of thousands of refugees
> from the most dangerous countries on Earth . . . people who believe
> women should be enslaved and gays put to death. [She] may be the
> most corrupt person ever to seek the presidency [and has] put forward
> the most radical immigration platform in the history of the United
> States [while]the first victims . . . will be poor African-American and
> Hispanic workers who need jobs. . . . Hillary also wants to spend hun-
> dreds of billions to resettle Middle Eastern refugees in the United
> States . . . will abolish the 2nd amendment [while her] massive taxation,
> regulation and open borders will destroy jobs and drive down wages
> for everyone (Trump 2016d).

A 2016 analysis of Trump's syntax revealed that he combined an adjec-
tive followed by someone's name ten times more than any other candidate as evidenced by his proclivity for using Twitter to launch personal
attacks on specific individuals, like "lightweight" Megyn Kelly, "little"
Marco Rubio, "low-energy" Jeb Bush, and "dopey" Bill Kristol (Tsur,
Ognyanova, and Lazer 2016). In order to grasp Trump's use of adjectives
through which he framed specific people Tsur and his colleagues developed a network, where they connected prominent individuals with the
adjectives to which they appeared proximate. "Nasty," for example, was
reserved for Hillary Clinton, Ted Cruz, and Marco Rubio, with Cruz
being the primary target. "Weak," on the other hand, was shared among
Jeb Bush, Clinton, Carly Fiorina, and Rubio. "Lightweight," while aimed
at multiple targets, was especially used against Rubio. Megyn Kelly and
Jon Stewart were "overrated." Pollster Frank Luntz was "wonderful" and
"great" (alluding to some good numbers Luntz predicted for Trump).
And finally, perhaps not surprisingly, the biggest recipient of adjectives
was Trump himself, who was associated with words such as "great,"
"beautiful," and "successful."

AN UNCONVENTIONAL BASE

In the end, it was his white base that most benefited Donald Trump. And of that base, his most enthusiastic supporters were white men across the board, with 54 percent of college-educated white men and 72 percent non-college-educated white men backing him. These white men and women voted like a minority group, according to one electoral analyst, coalescing on a mission to put him in the White House (Modhin 2016; see also Filipovic 2016 and M. Cooper 2016b).

Goldberg (2015) believes Trump represented the full emergence of a new Republican base created by Ronald Reagan: "They're still fired up by the core message of Reagan's first inaugural address in January 1981: 'Government is the problem.'" Trump took Reagan's "government is the problem" message and "stripped it down to its essence: They're all stupid. They're losers. I'm nothing like them. I'm great." Rhetorical strength promoted an ability to emphasize themes that resonated with his segment of the Republican party. For this base, partisan and traditional appeals to love of country and rejecting the concept of an interconnected international system ultimately gave way to a focus "not only on winning, but making sure that everyone else loses" (Ross 2015).

In Trump's campaign, there was no cohesive agenda or articulated plan for helping average Americans, which inspired him to speak to his "orphaned" base through a classic populism much in the same manner as "Napoleon Bonaparte and Julius Caesar before him: You got problems? Of course you do. Look at who's running things. Follow me—I know how to do things." Enter the "Freedom Kids," three adorable little girls who opened up Trump's campaign stop at a Tampa, Florida, rally. To the tune of the "Over There"—the "feel-good hit of trenches and mustard gas"—they invited the audience to join them in celebrating as America's enemies "face the music":

> *Cowardice*
> *Are you serious?*
> *Apologies for freedom, I can't handle this.*
> *When freedom rings, answer the call!*
> *On your feet, stand up tall!*
> *Freedom's on our shoulders, USA!*
> *Enemies of freedom face the music, c'mon boys, take them down*
> *President Donald Trump knows how to make America great*
> *Deal from strength or get crushed every time*

Billet (2016) observed at the time that although this was a "cartoon version of American nationalism," the "sheer absurdity" of which was "stunning," Trump's supporters would "love it and accuse anyone who doesn't of being a terrorist and a communist."

Mediation Strategies

While the use of social media as a campaign tool was not itself unique during the 2016 presidential campaign (see K.N. Smith 2011 and Vonderschmitt 2012) it was personalized differently by the candidates. Trump was unique by way of the sheer magnitude of his presence on social media. While the candidates' level of posting was about the same, public response was "far from equal." In every measurable category of user attention measured by a 2016 Pew Research study—Facebook shares, comments, and reactions, as well as Twitter retweets—the public responded to Donald Trump's social media updates more frequently on average than to either Bernie Sanders's or Hillary Clinton's posts (*Candidates Differ in Their Use* 2016). For example, Trump's posts on Twitter were retweeted almost 6,000 times on average compared with just over 1,500 for Clinton and almost 2,500 for Sanders. This may be due in part to Trump's higher number of followers. Near the time of publication of the study, Donald Trump had almost 10 million followers on Twitter compared with Clinton's 7 million and Sanders's 3 million, while on Facebook, 9 million followed Trump's official page, about double the number who followed either Clinton's or Sanders's sites. In addition, Trump's Facebook posts and Twitter feeds also pointed readers more frequently to news media. Almost 80 percent of his posts with links directed followers to articles from large national or international media organizations such as Fox News and the *Daily Mail*, as well as more niche sites like the conservative magazine *The American Spectator*. Trump never linked to his campaign site in a Facebook post "which seems to be in line with Trump's general strategy of focusing on media appearances and rallies during this period, rather than volunteers or donations":

> Trump's unique engagement with the public on Twitter stands apart not just from the other 2016 candidates but also from past presidential campaigns. In 2012, the candidates' social media outreach offered little engagement with the public. Just 3% of Obama's tweets during the period studied were retweets of the public—and most of these were posted during a live Twitter Q&A. Romney rarely used the retweet functionality and never retweeted the public (*Candidates Differ in Their Use* 2016).

Digital Assassination

Donald Trump successfully utilized a rhetorically sophisticated program of strategic digital character assassination against Hillary Clinton. While, arguably, most political campaigns involve attempts to discredit the "opposition candidate," this complex tactic lowers the bar considerably. Attributes of character assassination include an agency which involves doublespeak, raising false accusation, fostering rumors, spreading innuendo, or misinforming others about an opponent's morals and integrity. The persuasive technique is employed to manage information in order to secure a "competitive advantage" over an opponent. To that end, digital assassination could involve dissemination of propaganda or disinformation to demoralize the "other" or manipulate a public. In this way, the perceived quality of any "responding information" is impeached and opportunities for information collection by the opponent are severely hampered:

> A common disinformation tactic is to mix some truth and observation with false conclusions and lies. It can be used through falsifications that involve exaggeration, misleading half-truths, or factual manipulation to present an untrue picture of the opponent (Samoilenko 2016; see also Torrenzano and Davis 2011).

A digital "attacker" seeks to hurt the victim politically, morally, socially, or psychologically in order to remove that individual from a competition or sway public opinion. As such, it is an intentional discursive behavior designed to "seriously damage" the reputation or character of another person with the ultimate goal being to harm and reduce public support for the "victim." Such a technique would be useful to a politician because it would

> increase their chances of being elected by making exaggerated claims about the benefits that everyone will get if they win. On the other hand, they increase their chances by exaggerating the dire consequences if they lose. Character assassination in this case could become an effective means to alarm or scare some voters and sway them into a desirable course of action (Shiraev 2010).

To illustrate, Donald Trump successfully damaged the Democratic frontrunner's reputation with the "unfelt cuts" of paralipsis, a rhetorical device which allowed Trump to repeatedly make false accusations and spread false rumors against Clinton without a fear of consequences. For example, he could publicly tweet and communicate untrue Facebook statements about Hillary Clinton that he could later disavow — without ever having to take responsibility for his words (Mercieca 2016; see also Chozick and Parker 2016). The reliance on such devices enabled him to re-frame his lack of credentials and unpolished discourse, normally a drawback in presidential communication, to instead authenticate him as anti-establishment to his disenfranchised primarily white working-class base.

Trump's digital communication handlers were uniquely skilled at manipulating social media through using voter databases to "microtarget" his disenfranchised portion of the electorate. These included one supplied by Cambridge Analytica, with its 5,000 "data points" on 220 Americans including personality profiles on all of them and the RNC's enhanced "Voter Vault" which claimed to have data that included close to eight million data points on nearly 200 million voters. In addition, the Trump campaign had custom designed their own microtargeting "Project Alamo," derived in part from millions of small donors to the campaign and email addresses from rallies, merchandise sales, and even text messages sent to Donald Trump's campaign. To illustrate:

> Trump's digital operation [was] launched by buying $2 million in Facebook ads—his entire budget at the time. [The director] uploaded all known Trump supporters into the Facebook advertising platform and . . . matched actual supporters with their virtual doppelgangers and then . . . parsed them by race, ethnicity, gender, location, and other identities and affinities. From there he [found] people with interests and qualities similar to those of his original cohort and developed ads based on those characteristics. . . . Eventually [the campaign] was reportedly spending $70 million a month on digital advertising, most of it on Facebook [which] also netted Trump $250 million in donations. While it may not have created individual messages for every voter, the Trump campaign used Facebook's vast reach, relatively low cost, and rapid turnaround to test tens of thousands and sometimes hundreds of thousands of different campaign ads. . . . And this was just Facebook (Halpern 2017).

Trump also benefitted from his digital team's targeting use of Twitter; Wikileaks, "fake news" generators like Breitbart; and by "Twitter bots," automated Twitter accounts at least some of which are thought to have emanated from Russia and at least one thousand of which the neo-Nazi website Daily Stormer claimed to have created. Other digital innovations included the purchasing of all YouTube ad space on election day in which Trump's campaign ran brief videos, each hosted by a different surrogate, and the use of Facebook's "dark posts" which enabled Trump to attack Clinton with targeted negative ads that "flew below the public radar" as part of the Trump team's concerted effort to dissuade potential Clinton voters from showing up at the polls. One such ad targeted "idealistic white liberals"—primarily Bernie Sanders's supporters; another was directed at young women through a "procession of women who claimed to have been sexually assaulted by Bill Clinton and harassed by the candidate herself," and a third was aimed at African Americans in urban centers, traditional sites of high Democratic voter turnout. One dark post featured a *South Park*-like animation narrated by Hillary Clinton, using then President Bill Clinton's anti-crime initiative in which she called certain young black men "super predators" who had to be brought "to heel."

In the words of one Trump senior campaign official as these ads were being disseminated: "We've modeled this [dark post campaign]. It will dramatically affect her ability to turn these people out" (quoted in Halpern 2017). According to Bouie (2015), Donald Trump's rhetorical talent derived not from a cohesive ideology but from an ethos as "an opportunist who borrows freely from both parties." Once his disaffected Rust Belt base was identified, Trump's digital team laser-focused on those voters in the rural areas of Michigan, Wisconsin, and Pennsylvania during the last phase of their campaign. And the strategy worked. Hillary Clinton received roughly 70,000 votes fewer in Detroit than Mr. Obama did in 2012; she lost Michigan by just 12,000 votes. In Wisconsin, she received roughly 40,000 votes fewer than Mr. Obama did, and she lost the state by just 27,000 while turnout in majority African-American precincts was down 11 percent from four years ago (David Plouffe, Barack Obama's 2008 campaign manager, cited in Halpern 2017).

By January 2017, while the majority of Americans—57 percent—agreed that Russia tried to interfere in the 2016 presidential election in order to defeat Clinton and support Trump, just over half of Republicans—53 percent—refused to accept the conclusions of U.S. intelligence agencies that Russia tried to interfere in the 2016 election at all (Dutton et al. 2017). Despite reliable information from some of the most credible sources for the information regarding Russia's digital assault, over half of Trump's base chose to share in his vision that the Russian story was simply more "fake news" from a liberal media still infatuated with Hillary Clinton (see Kiely 2017 and Wilts 2017).

THE OUTCOME: UNITED WITH HIM AGAINST HER

On a variety of issues, Trump appeared to "take a page from Bernie Sanders's playbook" as he vowed to increase minimum wage; suggested the wealthy might pay higher taxes than he had originally proposed, and attacked Hillary Clinton "from the left" on national security and Wall Street. According to Parker and Martin (2016), Donald Trump mirrored Bernie Sanders on a variety of populist issues, in order to win working-class Democrats during a final showdown with Hillary Clinton, not Sanders. Although the Republican front-runner coined the dismissive nickname of "Crazy Bernie," he still borrowed campaign lessons from Sanders, whom he frequently also praised from the stump, on how to run against Hillary Clinton. He also rhetorically framed Sanders as a sort of co-conspirator in their joint campaign against the Democratic front-runner. As an example, during Trump's remarks at the Republican National Convention in Cleveland, Sanders became a source of "expertise" to validate his criticism of Hillary Clinton:

> America is far less safe—and the world far less stable—than when Obama made the decision to put Hillary Clinton in charge of America's foreign policy. I am certain it is a decision he truly regrets. Her bad instincts and her bad judgment—something pointed out by Bernie Sanders—are what caused so many of the disasters unfolding today (Trump 2016c).

Later in the same speech, Bernie Sanders was portrayed by Trump as a victim of Clinton after which the Republican makes an appeal to Sanders's supporters to unite together against the woman who had wronged and defeated their candidate:

> Nobody knows the system better than me, which is why I alone can fix it. I have seen firsthand how the system is rigged against our citizens, just like it was rigged against Bernie Sanders—he never had a chance. But his supporters will join our movement, because we are going to fix the system so it works fairly and justly, for each and every American (Trump 2016c).

Again, during the August 2016 New York City speech, Sanders was mentioned to credential Trump's view that Clinton was an unfit candidate:

> Hillary Clinton wants to be president. But she doesn't have the temperament, or, as Bernie Sanders said, the judgment to be president. She believes she is entitled to the office. Her campaign slogan is "I'm with her." You know what my response to that is I'm with you: the American people. She thinks it's all about her (Trump 2016d).

Trump also indicated an opposition to free trade could centerpiece his general election campaign. This approach suggested he was anticipating that the 2016 campaign would not be decided in diverse states that represented the "face of a changing nation" such as Colorado or Virginia, but in the more "heavily white Rust Belt," where blaming trade deals for manufacturing job losses created important themes for both Sanders and Trump during their primaries there. Before campaigning in Oregon, Trump praised Sanders for highlighting Clinton's ties to the country's largest financial corporations and repeated what had become a rally theme for Sanders: "She's totally controlled by Wall Street" (Trump quoted in Parker and Martin 2016).

Donald Trump accepted the Republican nomination for president in July 2016, and assured that the United States under his reign would "be a country of generosity and warmth." He revealed he had "joined the political arena so that the powerful can no longer beat up on people that cannot defend themselves." He also spoke directly to the "rage" of those Democrats who felt betrayed by Hillary Clinton, reminding them of her "base instincts" and "bad judgment." And he did so with the same "loud, insistent, uncivil and effective voice" with which he had so often spoken to his Republican supporters during the primaries. The only difference this time was that Trump made certain to remind those now "even more" disenfranchised Democrats that his criticism of Clinton had been corroborated by none other than Bernie Sanders (Trump 2016c; see also Stuckey 2016).

FIVE

Post-Election Rhetorical Behavior of Sanders and Trump

The political spectrum is rarely a straight line. Perhaps counterintuitively, the extreme far-right and far-left are often not diametric opposites of one another but united through a common enemy and the way they approach the change each seeks. This is arguably the case with the extreme "left" and extreme "right" personifications of the Democratic and Republican Parties, as represented by Bernie Sanders and Donald Trump in the 2016 presidential campaign. Sanders's and Trump's races were united through a common enemy, Hillary Rodham Clinton, and in the way they approached the change each sought her defeat (Pazienza 2016). Fitzpatrick (2016) suggests that although they were running for different parties, Sanders and Trump shared supporters who were "not so much attracted by a policy platform as by a personality and an attitude and a dissatisfaction about the ways things are."

Shared Ground

On both sides of the political spectrum, during and after the 2016 campaign, Americans were expressing their impatience with and general dislike of "career politicians" and even political parties as untrustworthy or corrupted by Washington insiders (Nevius 2016). It appears that Bernie Sanders and Donald Trump jointly benefitted from and continued to exploit this distrust of mainstream politics and politicians with their ongoing divisive and partisan appeals to their bases. On first look, by the time of the February New Hampshire primary, there was not much in common between the GOP winner Donald Trump and Democratic winner Bernie Sanders. Trump was a billionaire business mogul, Sanders a career politician. Trump's "personal favorability" was the lowest of all candidates on either side; Sanders's was the highest. But they shared a base of "oppressed" and indignant voters in search of "a powerful authority figure to fix everything using the power of the government." Because independents could register as "undeclared" in New Hampshire and then vote in either party's primary, the Vermont senator's campaign was well aware that some of their supporters were wavering between Sanders and Trump, primarily because the two candidates were "not that different on policy." Ben Shapiro (2016) details some of their discourse in the run-up to the primary. Both candidates presented as anti-establishment heroes who attacked Wall Street. Trump maintained:

> It's special interests' money, and this is on both sides. This is on the Republican side, the Democrat side, money just pouring into commercials. These are special interests, folks. These are lobbyists. These are people that don't necessarily love our country. They don't have the best interests of the country at heart (Trump quoted in Shapiro, 2016).

Sanders was just as certain:

> We have sent a message that will echo from Wall Street to Washington, from Maine to California, and that is that the government of our great country belongs to all of the people and not just a handful of wealthy campaign contributors, and their Super PACs (Sanders quoted in Shapiro, 2016).

Each also shared views that trade was a zero-sum game at which America was losing. Sanders considered trade with China as "catastrophic." Trump noted that he and Sanders mirrored each other on the topic: "The one thing we very much agree on is trade. We both agree that we are getting ripped off by China, by Japan, by Mexico, everyone we do business with."

Both candidates wanted to undo Obamacare. Trump was unclear on its replacement but promised he would stop the "insurance companies . . . getting rich on Obamacare" and ensure "we're going to take care of the people on the street dying." Sanders was more specific:

> Twenty-nine million Americans should not remain uninsured, an even greater number remain under-insured with large deductibles and co-payments. We should not be paying by far the highest prices in the world for prescription drugs at a time—listen to this, when the top three drug companies in this country made $45 billion dollars in profit last year. That is an obscenity, and let me tell you something. When we make it to the White House, the pharmaceutical industry will not continue to rip-off the American people (Sanders quoted in Shapiro).

Both also endorsed Trump's vow to "enshrine" programs like Medicare and Social Security. And while Trump ran on a promise to enforce a strict anti-illegal immigration policy, Sanders historically opposed illegal immigration on the basis of driving down American wages:

Bring in all kinds of people, work for $2 or $3 an hour, that would be great for them. Real immigration reform puts the needs of working people first—not wealthy globetrotting donors. This is straight from the Trump playbook (Sanders quoted in Shapiro).

They shared common ground when discussing foreign policy. Trump insisted he opposed the war in Iraq and that military spending should be cut and Russia should deal with ISIS. Sanders promised:

As president I will defend this nation, but I will do it responsibly. I voted against the war in Iraq, and that was the right vote. While we must be relentless in combating terrorists who would do us harm, we cannot, and should not be the policeman of the world. Nor should we bear the burden of fighting terrorism alone. In the Middle East, the United States must remain part of an international coalition sustained by nations in the region that have the means to protect themselves. Together we must, and will, destroy ISIS, but we should do it in a way that does not put our young men and women in the military into perpetual warfare in the quagmire of the Middle East (Trump and Sanders quoted in B. Shapiro 2016).

Healy (2016b) maintains that Hillary Clinton's politically safe message of "I'm a progressive who gets results" was far less compelling to a frustrated and disenfranchised electorate than the distinctly outsider messages of Bernie Sanders's "political revolution" and Donald Trump's "Make America Great Again." Fitzpatrick (2016) noted that both described the North American Free Trade Agreement and the Trans-Pacific Partnership Agreement with the same word: "disaster." They were also "isolationists" as evidenced by harsh criticism of Capital Hill donors and lobbyists; and shared disgust about the country's economy, particularly regarding middle-class and working-class families.

Their post-election behavior continued to evidence a peculiarly symbiotic partnership through a politics of pessimism. Both still occupied their "angry candidate" mode and pursued the same scapegoats they had chased during their campaigns. Sanders continued to blame greedy billionaires for the problems of the middle class and the poor. Trump blamed dangerous immigrants and Muslims (Charen 2016). They still argued mainstream politics and elected leaders were corrupt; that honest and hard-working Americans (only voters who supported Sanders or Trump) were being deceived and mistreated; that "someone" else was going to "pay" for the mistreatment/"crony capitalism," and spoke words to assure their "orphaned" electorates remained "mad as hell" (Fagen 2016; see also Cupp 2016 and Mahbubani 2016). Trump was still continuing to "protect" Sanders from Hillary Clinton when he lashed out at the former Secretary of State from behind his presidential podium with accusations that she had been "unfair to Bernie" when she had been "allowed to collude" with the Democratic party in the presidential pri-

mary to defeat Bernie Sanders (Korade and Watkins 2017). Once he was
certain that Clinton was the Democratic nominee, Trump began to discursively occupy the "outsider" space which had once belonged to Sanders, still maintaining a "divided together against Hillary Clinton" ethos.

Clinton expected to inherit the nomination without serious opponents. Joe Biden and John Kerry didn't run, deferring to the Clintons'
power in the party and to Hillary Clinton's claim that it was "our time"
as women to win the presidency—an appeal that, surprisingly, bored
younger women. As an independent, Sanders lacked such loyalty. His
campaign addressed the displaced and disempowered, claiming Clinton
was the problem not the solution. In response, after winning Super Tues-
day, Clinton declared: "We will defend all our rights . . . civil rights and
voting rights, human rights . . . women's rights and worker's rights . . .
LGBT rights and rights for people with disabilities!" Such pluralistic appeals to civil rights across the board, including those of workers, women,
and voters, made it difficult for her campaign to present a national mission with which even Sanders's supporters could identify. That she did
proved Donald Trump's complaint that Democrats were so busy "kow-
towing" to minorities they neglected the white majority and the nation's
need for consensus. Having catered to the millennial and minority sensibility in the spring, Hillary Clinton missed the mainstream, failing to
recalibrate for the fall.

Divergent Strategies

There may be over simplified and even misleading caricatures of what
were in fact two quite distinct candidacies as well as Sanders's and
Trump's enactments of post-election behaviors. Some of Donald Trump's
immunity from criticism was shared by the other "outsider" in the race,
Sanders, whose more "rabid supporters" became angry when their candidate received negative press or criticism (Nevius 2016). However, unlike
Trump, Sanders was not a flip-flopper but was instead challenged with
having to defend some positions that were not always in keeping with his
other progressive policies. Nor did Sanders tell outright lies.

In addition, it can also be argued that, despite his long-standing criticism of the "ruling class" and his self-framing as an "outsider," Sanders—unlike Trump—was nonetheless a professional politician who ran
an effective campaign (Troy 2016; see also *Research: Media Coverage* 2016).
He was also a part of the American political establishment, having held
elective office for more than three decades, including almost 25 years
serving in the House and then the Senate. While Sanders, a self-described
(if not textbook) socialist, was on record as incessantly criticizing the
"billionaire class," he rarely actually attacked other politicians directly or
by name while Trump often attacked political rivals and in distinctly
personal terms. Although many joint strategies followed both into post-

election arenas, including holding firm to their original voters, there were some variations. Sanders remained true to his persistent message while Trump as president-elect and then president relied on "his outsized personality" to "add rhetorical bluster" in order to mask a dearth of policy specifics. This may have been a strategic behavior on Trump's part as it allowed his supporters, many of whom were not initially part of his original base, "across the Republican ideological spectrum, and perhaps beyond, to claim him as one of their own" (Dickinson 2015).

Furthermore, Sanders's and Trump's proponents may have looked at "the dragon from different vantage points" and saw "fundamentally different dangers." Blow (2016c) argues Trump's supporters shared his vision of a country in decline; an out of control and incompetent government; with immigrants as threats to their livelihoods and lives; and a culture "hamstrung by political correctness." Conversely, while Sanders's acolytes agreed that democracy was under siege from oligarchic corporate and political powerbrokers, they were more concerned that the country had failed to keep up with other democracies on social welfare issues including economic equality, taxation, health care, and education and "has gone completely off the rails" on others such as criminal justice and mass incarceration. It may also be that Sanders differed from Trump, as he told MSNBC's Andrea Mitchell, in that he avoided "demagoguery" and "racist attacks" and tried instead to "talk about the reality facing the American people." Trump would probably argue the point as he no doubt believed he was talking about that reality as well. Still, their policy agendas were, in many respects, miles apart (Goldberg 2015).

THE DEBATE-THAT-NEVER-WAS

The idea for a debate with Trump, sans Clinton, was generated personally by Sanders when talk show host Jimmy Kimmel's producers contacted his campaign for a question to ask Donald Trump (Dovere and Debenedetti 2016). There was blowback to Sanders's courting of Trump in this manner. In Clymer's (2016) view the "quick Twitter nod" Sanders sent to Donald Trump after learning that the Republican front-runner had agreed to his offer was "both surprising in the blatant misogyny of the moment and unsurprising." Rather than a demonstration of an open democratic process in order to discuss issues, Sanders's actions were about preserving his "massive ego and that of his base" as well as a demonstration of:

> [Sanders's] petulance in the midst of a candidacy that has won less total votes, less states, and less delegates than his opponent, a woman who is the only person in this race with a rightful claim to debate Donald Trump on the national stage (Clymer 2016).

In the end, Donald Trump pulled out of the debate with Bernie Sanders. Pazienza (2016) describes the short arc of the debate-that-did-not-happen as defined by Trump who "surprisingly both fed Sanders's ego and poured cold water on him." The Republican front-runner had second thoughts the day after clinching "his" party's nomination, stating that because "Crooked Hillary" would never allow Bernie Sanders to win now that he was the "presumptive Republican nominee" it seemed "inappropriate" that he would "debate the second-place finisher" (Trump quoted in Millward 2016).

Nonetheless, Sanders remained adamant that American voters should have the benefit of watching and listening to Donald Trump and Bernie Sanders engage in the presidential debate he had personally arranged, despite the fact that one of the two would-be debaters had virtually no chance of ever running against the other for the presidency. Bernie Sanders was still campaigning:

> There is a reason why in virtually every national and state-wide poll I am defeating Donald Trump, sometimes by very large margins and almost always by far larger margins than Secretary Clinton. There is a reason for that reality and the American people should be able to see it up front in a good debate and a clash of ideas (Sanders quoted in Millward 2016).

The Bernie Pivot

Despite the obvious differences between Bernie Sanders and Donald Trump and their enactments of running for the presidency, the two men did have common ground between them, at least in one of their minds. During an MSNBC townhall appearance, host Mika Brzezinksi described to Donald Trump a candidate who was considered a political outsider, tapped into the anger of the electorate, delivered a populist message, and drew thousands of new voters to their rallies. When she queried, "Who am I describing?" Trump responded "you're describing Donald Trump (quoted in Fitzpatrick 2016). Yet, despite their mutual appeals to seriously disenfranchised voters, Trump and Sanders did utilize different discourses to persuade each of their unique portions of their angry "orphaned" base.

Beginning with the 2015 announcement of his intention to compete against Hillary Clinton for the Democratic nomination, Bernie Sanders was transparent in communicating what would continue to be a significant difference between his campaign and that of Donald Trump, a refusal to go negative and personally attack Clinton:

> Let's be clear. This campaign is not about Bernie Sanders. It is not about Hillary Clinton. It is not about Jeb Bush or anyone else. This campaign is about the needs of the American people and the ideas and proposals that effectively address these needs. As someone who has never run a

negative political ad in his life, my campaign will be driven by issues and serious debate; not political gossip, not reckless personal attacks or character assassination (Sanders 2015b).

Sanders's "soak the rich" populism resonated with voters occupying the most progressive wing of the Democratic Party and drew particularly strong support among highly educated, and often wealthy, white voters as well as college students. His ideological brand was relatively narrow, and his appeals were less rigorously targeted to racial and ethnic minorities or centrist, lower-income Democrats. Sanders's progressive agenda and even his basic message had essentially been the same in 2015 and throughout 2016 through the nomination convention, since before entering the House in 1991. Finally, his approach to policies in general was rooted in a fundamental endorsement of more government as a prerequisite to addressing America's problems (Dickinson 2015).

His post-primary behavior was driven by political anger, directed against Clinton's policies and position as a political "insider." After learning that she had surpassed the "magic number" of delegates needed to clinch the Democratic Party's nomination, Sanders predicted and promised a contested convention at which he would "take our fight for social, economic, racial and environmental justice" (Sanders quoted in Reston 2016). He also vowed to stay in the presidential race promising his "on edge and angry" base that he would "continue to fight for every vote and every delegate" (Sanders quoted in Barbaro and Alcindor 2016). Bruni (2016) maintains that Sanders's "graceless losing" was due in part to the election's "particular characters." In Sanders's case, "when you're not just a man but a revolution, you can never quit the fight or flee the front." But Bernie Sanders's refusal to endorse Hillary Clinton revealed "there's more at work" as well:

> The refusal to grant victors legitimacy bundles together so much about America today: the coarseness of our discourse; the blind tribalism coloring our debates; the elevation of individualism far above common purpose; the ethos that everybody should and can feel like a winner on every day (Bruni 2016).

Wade (2016) describes Sanders's post-primary organization as a "walking dead" campaign, within which Sanders was a "zombie candidate" who couldn't win the nomination

> but [who could] squander vast amounts of time and slowly chip away at the front-runner. Some of the damage is obvious—the endless series of public dents in the candidate's reputation; some are subtle, noticeable in ways that perhaps only political operatives can appreciate [such that] continuing to contest a primary after your path to victory disappears is not healthy; it actively hinders your would be-partisan ally (see also Peters and Rappeport 2016).

With Trump essentially guaranteed to become the Republican nominee, the general election public was beginning to "tune in." Sanders was not helping them find their way to Clinton:

> At a time when voters could be comparing Trump and Secretary Clinton, the presumptive nominees, they're instead seeing Clinton take shrapnel not just from the Republicans, but from Sanders. [At this point] it would be better for the Democratic Party if Clinton could focus on the asymmetric political warfare to come from Trump—which she could do right now if she didn't have to maintain a second front to battle a primary opponent who cannot win (Wade 2016).

Though he personally—albeit indirectly—ultimately endorsed Hillary Clinton after she won the Democratic nomination, much of Sanders's "revolutionary" base held fast to the idea that that the party establishment had stacked the deck and rigged the primaries to make sure she won (Sanders 2016d). The complaints grew louder after Clinton lost to Trump, who, like Sanders, declared himself a candidate of the working man (J. Williams 2017). As Clinton faded from public view, Bernie Sanders appeared to "not only still be here—he's everywhere," accompanied by members of progressive organizations and operatives who rallied around his presidential campaign—"the Bernie Mafia," as they called themselves (Seitz-Wald 2016c).

For instance, during a speech delivered a week after the presidential election to a packed auditorium of college students, Sanders rallied his still-fervent base with a "tough-love" vision for the future of the Democratic Party in which not only was he the hero but Hillary Clinton appeared, by way of innuendo, as the villain of his story and reason for Trump's victory:

> I think a lot of people gave up on the Democratic Party in terms of standing up for working people and then said, 'OK, I'm going to go with this guy.' Ordinary people have got to know that the Democratic Party has the guts to stand up to some very powerful people today whose greed is destroying the middle class and working class of this country. And if we can't do that, I don't see much of a future for the Democratic Party (Sanders quoted in Seitz-Wald 2016c).

The following day, he spoke at "what felt like a campaign rally" organized by a pro-Sanders union. The audience waved "Bernie 2020" signs that the union had printed, and he shared the stage with friends from the union and his campaign. Again, while not mentioning Clinton directly, she was nonetheless clearly blamed for the state of the nation's political culture. Moreover, through his not-so-subtle but clearly successful rhetorical use of innuendo, Bernie Sanders offered himself as the savior for his orphaned and partisan audience:

> I'm not here to blame anybody, not to criticize anybody, but facts are facts. When you lose the White House to the least popular candidate in

the history of America, when you lose the Senate, when you lose the House, and when two-thirds of governors in this country are Republicans, it is time for a new direction for the Democratic Party (Sanders quoted in Seitz-Wald 2016c).

Kilgore (2016) reports that there were many ways Bernie Sanders could have helped "clear the air." For instance, he could have told his base that, while there was much about the Democratic nomination process that should be changed, no one had "stolen" the nomination from him or them. That Sanders chose to remain silent demonstrated that both he and his base should have known "better than to conclude" what had "been a brilliant and important campaign by turning it into an extended temper tantrum." Ultimately, although Bernie Sanders may have imagined a post-election legacy where he would be memorialized as "The Leader of the Revolution," it is just as likely that he will be remembered as "The Spoiler" for his role in electing a president "hostile to liberalism, unafraid of demonizing minorities and epitomizing a killer instinct that makes Clintonian triangulation look naïve" (Troy, 2016).

The Donald Pivot

Post-convention Donald Trump waged his campaign as the Republican nominee as he had during the primaries, but with additional emotional rhetoric aimed at framing his angry electorate as not only abandoned by elite politicians (Clinton) but, worse, caught up in the corrupt mechanism which "spawned" Clinton: the democratic system itself. His "scorched earth" and "take-no-prisoners" mashup of hate rhetoric with fervent and powerful motivational "rhetorical" talk was an exigence which was addressed by push-back. Personal rather than political anger embedded in a context of partisan division was a cornerstone of Donald Trump's candidacy. While his policies were generally undeveloped at best, he nonetheless fed his disgruntled and "abandoned" followers:

vague, morning-mirror affirmations like "make America great again" and endless "winning," while largely avoiding particulars and parrying fact-checkers and his own history of inconsistencies. And yet, the people who support him, angry at the establishment, their own party, America itself, don't really care. He has touched their frustration and they feel reflected in his brutishness (Blow 2016a).

Trump's stance on the issues appeared to be more diffuse and difficult to define than Sanders's, not least because it often seemed that he filled in the details as his candidacy progressed and, later, through post-election behavior. This allowed him to draw support across the ideological spectrum of the Republican Party, a fact that helped explain why pundits had and still have trouble labeling him ideologically. Some claimed he was a moderate, citing his willingness to raise taxes on the rich, and his unwillingness to cut Social Security benefits. But on other issues, such as immigration or combating the Islamic State group, he adopted much more conservative positions.

Donald Trump's literal and rhetorical political behavior frequently seemed, both pre-and post-election, more reactionary and ideologically ungrounded than anchored in any concrete ideology, as foreshadowed by him in 1987: "When you're dealing, and that's what I am, I'm a dealer, you don't go in with plans. You go in with a certain flexibility. And you sort of wheel and deal" (Trump 1987, 2015). As a result, Trump's ideological base was expansive in that it anchored broader but was perhaps not quite as deeply attached as it might have been if he had not opted for such fluidity. This is in part because when Trump said/says "I will (fill in the solution)" it was/is not always clear how he proposed to do so (Dickinson 2015).

Azari (2014) argues that the shift toward more frequent and partisan mandate rhetoric has not only contributed to a decline in the status of the presidency but also resulted in the need for a president, once elected, to focus much less on consensus building and increasingly on base-driven defensive and partisan rhetoric about "the promises I made in my campaign" and "the reasons I was elected." Within a few months of his ascension to president, Donald Trump was essentially in a rhetorical "inversion of the permanent campaign" mode, wherein he continued referencing campaign promises and issues rather than speak about how he was going to address them. In May 2017, Trump said "I hate to see anything that divides," when asked about his view on the appointment of a special counsel to investigate whether his own aides were involved in Russian efforts to swing the 2016 election. He insisted he had nothing to do with the offense, and that it was a ruse by a small number of entrenched politicians who were trying to shake him from his great goal of bringing the country together: "whether it's Russia or anybody else, my total priority, believe me, is the United States of America" (quoted in Dovere 2017).

A substantial portion of his post-election rhetorical behavior continued to be informed by a personal anger. To illustrate, he publicly disparaged judges whose rulings he did not like, using terms like "disgraceful," "so political," and "so-called judge." "Presidents have criticized judicial decisions," said Ryan Crocker, executive professor at Texas A&M and a career United States ambassador, but such personalized anger from a sitting president was "abnormal because he is criticizing the judges themselves." His post-election discourse has also been characterized by falsehoods which he publicly shares, often through tweets, about otherwise indisputable events and verifiable information. Trump has intentionally distorted or clearly lied about some significant and verifiable facts, including the number of illegal voters in the 2016 election and the number of people who attended his inauguration. When asked about the correct numbers, Trump and some of his surrogates have dismissed such data as "fake news" or trivialized them as "alternative facts." According to Jennifer Hochschild, chair of the Department of Government at Harvard, "All politicians lie and stretch the truth" but Trump's behavior is "extreme" in that "it depends on how many people believe him" (quoted in Bui, Miller, and Qualey 2017).

Trump's secretary of state, Rex Tillerson, has criticized the president's tweets as undermining United States's foreign policy objectives, and has chafed when asked about the effect of Trump's tweets on conducting diplomacy, noting that he often had to deal with the undermining effects of presidential tweets that contradict his policy statements (cited in Kosinski and Gaouette 2017). When the August 2017 category four hurricane came ashore in Texas, Donald Trump continued to tweet in a way that journalist Jeff Greenfield argued "no other president would" and that was "simply not normal" and reflected the "bizarre" way Trump was handling his presidency. Instead of speaking encouraging words to those in immediate danger and providing guidance and leadership to steer the country through the first natural disaster it had experienced "on his watch," he turned to social media to complain to the public about tax reform and promoted a supporter's book. Referring to the president's relentless and unfiltered use of social media in general and Twitter in particular, editor-in-chief of *USAToday* Joanne Lipman argued that the press corps should "separate what's news from what's chatter." *Huffington Post's* editor-in-chief Lydia Polgreen says Trump's tweets "seem totally, completely outside of what you would expect of a president dealing with a disaster." Polgreen asserts that Trump's inappropriate tweets indicate not only that he is "outside the news cycle" but also an "abdication of moral leadership" (quoted in *Trump's Tweets,* 2017).

In effect, anger rather than policy still drove Donald Trump's post-election discourse (Blow 2016a). He continued to target Hillary Clinton even after early and occasional acting as the "beneficent pardoner," maintaining he would not continue investigations into the Clintons, who were "nice people" and had "suffered so much" (quoted in Bordo 2017). As the newly anointed president-elect, Trump railed against Clinton, declaring her "guilty as hell" and deriding her supporters' criticism of how the FBI handled an investigation into her emails (*Donald Trump Reprises Campaign Attacks,* 2017). Five months into his presidency, the former Secretary of State was clearly still on the president's mind and perhaps his radar as he tweeted an anger-by-innuendo question: "Did Hillary Clinton ever apologize for receiving the answers to the debate? Just asking!" (quoted in Rhodan 2017). And Diamond (2017) suggests that Trump was "still reverting to his old social media habits" a few months later, when POTUS retweeted an edited video of the president of the United States swinging a golf club and appearing to hit his former presidential campaign rival Hillary Rodham Clinton in the back with a golf ball (Diamond 2017).

SIX

Wired-In Populism

The public's understanding of the president and presidential candidates emerges within a political environment constituted through mediated messages, digital discourses, and popular culture. McLuhan (1964) maintained political awareness was one export of an electronically constituted "global village" while Gray (2002) wondered if digital media might have a similar and accelerated effect. Despite concerns such as "ultratargeting" and an increasingly fragmented electorate, the United States appears to be fully immersed in a digitally driven and ongoing "postmodern political revolution" (Gronbeck 2004; see also, Anderson 2016). The 2016 presidential race demonstrated this "wired-in" populism through the campaigns of Bernie Sanders and Donald Trump, as they rhetorically enacted their agendas and digitally interacted with their respective disenfranchised publics. Both parties had established "an essential resource" to reach their general Democratic and Republican bases, that of a well-defined path to the presidency, which was exploited more successfully and "more clearly on the Republican side." Donald Trump "hopped the Maginot Line" set up by the Republican establishment "to protect its well-trampled path to the White House" to the extent that he was ultimately able to "march along, unfettered." Sanders's campaign wanted that as well: "the attention and processes that make a candidate viable in the eyes of more than just a few thousand people on Twitter." Both outsider candidates achieved that goal, albeit with different levels of success (Bump 2016a).

REVOLUTIONARY MEDIA

Presidential campaign rhetoric has been mediated through mass communication channels for over two hundred years. When George Washington was elected the first American president, he was the unanimous choice, receiving the votes of all 132 electors. The country experienced its "first exposure to a true campaign" during the second presidential election when John Adams ran successfully against Thomas Jefferson, the nominee of the first American political opposition party, the Democratic-Republicans. Still, their campaigns would likely be unrecognizable as such by contemporary Americans since both Adams and Jefferson had to comply with the public's opposition to overt and direct appeals for votes (Weiss 2012).

Direct Democracy

The 1800 election ushered in a "dark age of partisan journalism" (Weiss 2012) as Jefferson bested Adams in part by using the preferred mass medium of the era. He paid the editor of the *Richmond Examiner* to print anti-Federalist articles and to praise the efforts of Jefferson's party. The paper also printed accounts of Jefferson supporters' accusations against incumbent Adams of having a "hideous hermaphroditical character, which has neither the force and firmness of a man, nor the gentleness and sensibility of a woman." Perhaps one of the first mediated presidential campaign battles ensued when, in response, Adams's advisors produced a pamphlet which called Jefferson "a mean-spirited, low-lived fellow, the son of a half-breed Indian squaw, sired by a Virginia mulatto father" (*Running for President,* 2016; see also Pasley 2003).

Although the system of the presidential elections has remained a constant in American society, the methods of campaigning have changed dramatically since Thomas Jefferson's tenure. Prior to the spread of television's popularity, twentieth-century citizens and politicians alike were primarily involved in presidential politics by reading local newspapers and visiting the politicians face to face. Since the successful campaigns of Theodore Roosevelt and Woodrow Wilson "popular or mass rhetoric has become a principal tool of presidential governance" (Tulis 1987). Kernell and Jacobson (1987) report that presidents have generally enjoyed an advantage in press coverage over Congress throughout the twentieth century. By the 1930s President Franklin D. Roosevelt used the radio to connect with the American public. By 1960, Nixon and Kennedy had televised a debate which introduced "real events with a very different reality" by way of a mass-produced face-to-face politics channeled through televisions coast-to-coast (Ranney 1984). While newspapers still expanded their knowledge of presidential politics (see Rosenstiel, Mitchell, Purcell, and Rainie 2011) advances in technology extended citizens' participation in that they learned more information about the candidates and had easier access to them as well (*Political Processes and Television* 2017).

By the 2008 U.S. presidential election, then Senator Barack Obama began using social media to engage and empower volunteers, raising millions of dollars, the first to do so with that level of success, in that the work transferred into actual votes (Vonderschmitt 2012; see also Bell et al. 2013; Iyengar and Kinder 1987, 2010; Eilperin 2015). A distinct digitalized form of direct democracy began to emerge driven by increasing selective exposure to political information combined with a fragmentation of the public and decline of citizen exposure to political information.

It has been suggested that the twenty-first century has added "media democracy" in a "truly revolutionary form," which originated in partisan talk radio but has evolved in an unprecedented manner. While late-stage political democracy evolved over two centuries,

> the media equivalent took around two decades, swiftly erasing almost any elite moderation or control of our democratic discourse. The rise of the internet—an event so swift and pervasive its political effect is only now beginning to be understood—further democratized every source of information, dramatically expanded each outlet's readership, and gave everyone a platform. All the old barriers to entry—the cost of print and paper and distribution—crumbled (Sullivan 2016).

UNMEDIATED MESSAGES

Prior to the 1990s and the invention of digital media, partisan polarization had been "reinforced by the weakening of the establishment new media" which up until then had been a "critical component of democratic accountability." Most Americans received their news via a "handful of trusted television networks" while politicians relied on the press to get the public's attention, so they could "ill afford to alienate journalists." However, beginning in the 2000s, the media have become "increasingly polarized" with the domination of Fox News signaling the end of an era of partisan news.

Political rhetoric has essentially always tended to demonize the "other." However, what is missing in contemporary contexts is a "generous inclination" to frame political controversy as "rooted in reasonable or at least understandable disagreement, and to seek political reform through persuasive conversation and compromise." One primary reason for this is the echo-chamber effect of digital media, the seeking of news that simply confirms one's existing beliefs. Such "niche-y nature" cyber-mediated outlets encourage people only to listen to commentators who reinforce their prejudices and "fuel their self-righteousness." The "explosion" of the Internet, meanwhile, has made it increasingly easier for people to seek out news that confirms their existing beliefs to the extent that "in the new media age, everybody is an expert" (Mickey, Levitsky, and Way 2017; see also Ross 2015 and R. Williams 2014).

Differences from Traditionally Mediated Campaigns

An extensive Pew Research study revealed that, since 2000, the Internet has evolved from what had essentially been thought of by the public as a novelty medium accessed by just half of the American population to a resource "now used" by nearly 90 percent and a primary way for Americans to keep up with the news, events, and issues. By 2016, nearly two-thirds of Americans indicated they learned about the Clinton/Sanders/Trump election on the web. During the 2000 primary, while nearly a quarter of Americans obtained a portion of their campaign-related information from the Internet, only 6 percent identified it as their primary source for campaign news. During 2004, the first presidential election year in which the Internet played a major role, there were more "digital-native" news providers (*Digital News Developments* 2017).

However, they offered fewer voter interactivity opportunities than in 2000 while the majority had no links to external news organizations. Over half of the sites, including CNN, offered no audio or visual links while those that did were technologically less sophisticated than they were four years before. By 2008 all nineteen of the presidential candidates had visible digital profiles including websites, blogs, and the "new" social media formats. Websites, blogs, and social media were the hot new formats and opening a wide array of opportunities for voters to connect with candidates and more actively participate in the election process. Facebook, YouTube, Meetup, and Flickr served as connection points with voters while "MySpace ruled the pack." Still, the number of followers fell far short of the numbers during the 2016 race. Barack Obama was the only candidate to exceed 100,000; most had fewer than 40,000, while content on the majority of the presidential sites was still reliant primarily on mainstream media sources.

By 2012, the candidates' campaign communications spotlighted bypassing the filter of traditional media more than mastering changing technologies to get their message to the voters. To that end, the role of traditional news media was reduced to "newsworthy" stories generated by the campaigns themselves. Furthermore, gaps emerged between the campaigns' technological advancement and level of digital activity. Overall, the Obama campaign's activity outpaced Romney's. The Romney campaign put more emphasis on Facebook and blogs, while the Obama campaign was most active on Twitter. Constituents were encouraged to take on or offline action and also found multiple ways to adapt campaign news to their interests, particularly on Obama's webpage. Still, neither campaign directly attempted to digitally engage the public. Finally, both Romney and Obama often included links in their digital posts, but their campaign websites were still the focal points of digital activity. The 2016 presidential campaigns of Hillary Clinton, Bernie Sanders, and Donald Trump foregrounded social media platforms which mandated revisions of campaign websites. Each of their digital characters became leaner and less interactive compared with previous election cycles. In addition, each presented high-profile but very controlled social media "places" which offered their respective constituents "less ways to engage and take part" (*Digital News Developments* 2017).

While websites still served as information and organization hubs, they were less interactive than in 2012 with very controlled messages which left fewer opportunities for voters to engage with the campaigns in general, let alone the candidates ("Presidential candidates . . . " 2016). On Facebook, Clinton and Sanders mostly used links to highlight official campaign communications while Trump linked frequently to the news media. On Twitter, Trump stood out for retweeting "ordinary people" more often than Clinton or Sanders (though retweets were rare). Videos, meanwhile, appeared in about a quarter of Clinton's social media posts, compared with about one-in-ten of Trump's; Sanders used video far more on Facebook than on Twitter. Finally, on both platforms, when the candidates mentioned their opponents, Clinton and Trump focused on each other while Sanders was largely issue oriented.

Columnist Charles Blow (2016a) condemned the media for its complicity in the ascension of Donald Trump to the presidency, particularly "the way we and the candidate operated in a symbiotic relationship, exchanging cheap ratings for free publicity" (see also Mortensen 2017). Kreiss (2016) maintains that the 2016 presidential election "took shape in a different world from 2002 and 2014." Ultimately, it is likely that essentially all successful future political campaigns, regardless of party affiliation, must and will be "newly technology-intensive" as well as mindful that "digital, data, and analytics are at the forefront of contemporary electoral politics."

Obama and Trump's Digital Presidencies

By Inauguration Day 2009, Barack Obama's transition team had already updated Whitehouse.gov. During the next year, additional modifications in their digital communication arsenal included developing new methods to archive social media posts and access social media archives. They also created White House-specific accounts for Facebook, Twitter, and Flickr through which the presidency could inform and engage the public (Bereznak 2017). Eight years later, Donald Trump's administration had inherited a "vast infrastructure," ranging from a Snapchat account to a White House Facebook messenger bot. Trump's team also appeared to be utilizing their digital medium platforms for different purposes and with different outcomes than the previous "digital presidency":

> Early online decisions from Trump's camp—which include his signature Twitter rants, major policy announcements and an emphasis on Facebook Live broadcasts . . . hint at an action-based tone; a brutalist

unfinished aesthetic; and largely promotional motivations (Bereznak 2017).

Noticeable differences between the digital presidencies of Barack Obama and Donald Trump included the latter team's gutting of "issue" pages related to LGBT rights, civil rights, climate change, and the Affordable Care Act, as well as the Spanish-language portal. According to the former director of Obama's Office of Digital Strategy such actions "show a non-commitment to the presidency in the digital design and technical capacities that we really set a pretty easy precedent for" (Ashleigh Axios quoted in Bereznak 2017).

Another characteristic of Donald Trump's digital White House is that the administration's strategy for outreach on major platforms like Facebook, Twitter, and Instagram have "all but turned inward," toward Trump's personal accounts rather than administration "government-owned" and official social media accounts. As a result, Trump's personal social media accounts—most frequently Twitter—became main sources of information about major announcements from within the White House. For example, according to Clay Dumas, former chief of staff for the Office of Digital Strategy:

> The White House Twitter account is now just a retweet account of @realDonaldTrump. They're generating less content . . . that's a reflection of staffing, but it's also that they are very focused on content that comes straight from the president (quoted in Bereznak 2017).

This suggests that the Trump White House operationalized its digital presidency with little interest in meaningful engagement or conversations with the public about issues.

WIRED-IN DIGITAL POPULISM

A 2016 American Press Institute study reported that 69 percent of millennials received their news daily while 85 percent said that keeping up with the news was at least somewhat important to them (cited in Fromm 2016). Another 2016 study, The Millennial Impact Project, found that a majority of millennials had posted on social media about the issues they cared about and concluded:

> With millennials being 2.5 times more likely to be early adopters of technology than other generations, it is no surprise that social media is playing such a large role in this election. This is, after all, a generation where a majority agree their life feels richer because they are connected through social media (*Millennial Impact Report* 2016).

In the near future, a post-millennial generation will grow up and vote. Though many "Gen Z-ers" are still too young to vote, they are taking an interest in social issues at a younger age than many generations before them, including millennials. These "powerful consumers and global in-fluencers" are "overwhelmingly more accepting of diversity than genera-tions before them and expect their political leaders to talk their language" (Fromm 2016). It would therefore be expedient for future twenty-first-century American political candidates and leaders to engage through "Gen Z's" preferred medium (see also Rolfe 2016). Millennials in particu-lar seem to respond to the "wired-in populism" of contemporary cam-paigning. Bernie Sanders was perhaps given the biggest boost by this demographic and their preferred medium, as in "state-after-state" and often whether a win or not, "he carried youth vote by wide margins" (Blow 2016b).

DIRECT DEMOCRACY

Sanders

In Bump's view (2016a), the emergence of the Internet allowed candi-dates like Bernie Sanders to become viable in ways that they couldn't have before the advent of social media. For example, Sanders's massive small-donor fundraising capability was solely a function of technology: one-click contributions and text message replies. The emergence of the "BernieBro"—Sanders's sometimes "painfully energetic" base of support on the Internet—was a function of the ability of the web to create pockets of individuals with a shared focus and interest. It is telling that in most of the Democratic primaries and caucuses, Bernie Sanders consistently did far better with independents that vote in the Democratic primaries and caucuses. In many cases, nearly half of Sanders's support in each contest came from such voters rather than mainstream registered Demo-crats. By March 2016, in 8 of the 15 contests in which Sanders was a candidate, 40 percent or more of his support had come from independent voters. In at least three of the states—New Hampshire, Oklahoma, and Michigan—those independent votes likely handed Sanders his win (Bump 2016a).

A key strategy of Bernie Sanders's presidential campaign was a plan to use social media to get his message out to millions of people. Sanders maintained he preferred this approach because of "corporate media's" disinterest in covering many of the critical economic issues facing the country. Facebook and Twitter were his preferred digital media. By late 2015, over 500,000 people followed him on Twitter and several thousand more were being added daily while a million people had liked Sanders' Facebook page and close to 10,000 people a day were added (Kinzel 2015). Sanders maintained that social media had "revolutionized a whole lot of things and in many ways it works for us because the message that I have been advocating for many, many years is quite difficult to get through the corporate media" (Sanders quoted in Kinzel 2015).

Budowsky (2015) credits a "brilliant use of social media" by his campaign for the "World Series" levels of Sanders's mostly millennial-driven base who attended his rallies and funded his campaign. While his Internet presence was not as robust as Trump's, Bernie Sanders nonetheless was skilled at social media use. A May 2016 Twitter declaration of "game on" followed by "I look forward to debating Donald Trump in California before the June primary," received roughly 28,000 retweets while a Facebook post celebrating Native Americans received over 52,000 shares (*Candidates Differ in Their Use* 2016). Donald Trump may have had the biggest social media following of all of the 2016 presidential candidates, but Bernie Sanders kept his followers the most engaged, according to a study by social media analytics platform Captiv8. "It's the authentic nature of Sanders's posts and conversations," Captiv8 cofounder Krishna Subramanian said of his ability to inspire a reaction from supporters. "The way to make these platforms really successful is by having conversations with your audience, posting content that makes them want to engage" (quoted in Chaykowski 2016).

By the February 2016 New Hampshire primary, Sanders's team had fine-tuned its social media outreach to blanket Facebook and Instagram with an aggressive campaign focused particularly on millennials. During the run-up to the primary, Bernie Sanders oversaw the largest and most aggressive advertising campaigns ever undertaken by a political campaign on Facebook and Instagram platforms. From January 20 to February 1, his campaign reached more than 750,000 people on Facebook and Instagram, 85 percent of whom were in the millennial bracket (Corasaniti 2016).

Trump

Over the span of the four decades before he entered the 2016 presidential race, Donald Trump courted the American press to his personal and corporate advantage. However, as the presumptive Republican presidential nominee, he adopted a far different attitude toward the media. With incessant Twitter blasts as Donald Trump's preferred medium and message, sometimes without the advice of aides, Trump posted about what he had seen on television. "Trump's off-the-cuff tweets" dramatically "increased the amount of uncertainty in the world," particularly when his appointees and staff contradicted the tweeted positions according to Erica Chenoweth, professor of international studies at the University of Denver. Tom Ginsburg, professor of comparative and international law at the University of Chicago, echoed some of the language in Trump's tweets: "Bad! Sad!" (cited in Bui, Miller, and Quealy 2017).

Beginning with what had begun as an occasional tweet against report-ers or commentators of outlets which had displeased him, Trump ulti-mately accumulated a lengthy blacklist of news organizations banned from covering his campaign events. While more symbolic than practical, since journalists could enter most campaign events with the public, Trump still pursued his rhetorical bullying of the media. For example, during one press conference, he continued to air his grievances when he insisted "I've never seen more dishonest media than, frankly, the political media" and later tweeted that the "fake media" —a favorite metaphor for any news story Trump did not like— "is not my enemy, it is the enemy of the American people!" According to the *New York Times* Editorial Board, Donald Trump at various times banned *The Washington Post, Foreign Poli-cy, Univision, The New Hampshire Union Leader, The Des Moines Register, The Daily Beast, The Huffington Post, Fusion, Buzz Feed News,* and *Gawker* (2016).

Digital Assassination

Media coverage of Campaign 2016 exposed the "limits and ideological impotence" of at least a portion of the established media's "objectivity" myth. This was particularly evidenced by the different—in degree and slant—coverage of each candidate's character and behaviors. Frequently, what was offered to the public as "fair and balanced" well-argued news was instead evidence of faux-argument, particularly that of a "false equivalency" manifest through a frequently digitalized "both sides meme" (Alterman 2016; see also Vanden Heuve 2014). For example, the coverage of Clinton's emails and Trump's sexual assault allegations were often framed as equally substantial and serious examples of faults in the candidates' characters.

In actuality, the "relative importance" of the email scandal to Clin-ton's fitness for office was dwarfed by "the torrent of allegations" against the GOP nominee (Johnson 2016). In addition, while Trump received substantial negative coverage in the press, the negatives "did not stick to him with same adhesion" as they had to Hillary Clinton (Traister 2017). Certainly, the imbalance was not apparent only in the coverage of Trump and Clinton. Johnson (2016) believes the "most common and reliably dull" example of the media's tendency to create "false equivalences" be-tween candidates was the "take" that Donald Trump and Bernie Sanders were ideologically "simply two sides of the same coin" (see also Shapiro 2016). This was a popular story, particularly early in the campaign during the primaries, designed to make it easier for media outlets to reduce the complexities of the presidential campaign to the binaries of a "horse race" (see Alterman 2016 and Dovere 2016).

CANDIDATES AS "THE CHOSEN"

Regardless, the candidacy most affected by mainstream American media's default to a "both sides meme" mentality in their reporting was demonstrated most clearly through their coverage of Hillary Clinton when compared to that of either Sanders or Trump. A Harvard Kennedy School Shorenstein Center on Media, Politics and Public Policy study examined the news coverage during the 2015 "invisible primary," a crucial year-long and media-driven lead-up to the primaries during which candidates lay the groundwork for successful campaigns (Patterson 2016b). During this period, major news outlets covered Donald Trump "in a way that was unusual given his low polling numbers," giving him far more "good press" than "bad press." The Democratic race received less than half the cover of the Republican race. Furthermore, while Bernie Sanders's campaign was initially ignored, it ultimately was the most favorably covered of any of the top candidates. Conversely, Hillary Clinton's coverage was far more negative than any other candidate, with her "bad news" outpacing her "good news," usually by a wide margin.

During this "invisible primary" period, media-generated metanarratives emerged about Sanders, Trump, and Clinton which persisted throughout 2016. Sanders's storyline was that he "means what he says" and speaks "from what he believes" rather than what "the polls say is expedient." Trump became the "shoot-from-the-hip bully," given to "braggadocio and insulting and outrageous comments" but his storyline also portrayed him as the candidate who "had a finger on the anger felt by many middle- and lower-class white voters." Conversely, the metanarrative created for Hillary Clinton was a tale of a candidate who was perhaps the "best prepared for the presidency" because of experience and knowledge but was "difficult to like, overly calculating, and hard to trust" (Patterson 2016b).

These narrative discrepancies continued to emerge in a second Harvard Kennedy School Shorenstein Center report detailing media coverage during the 2016 presidential campaign through November 2016. The study concluded that Hillary Clinton had continued to receive far more negative coverage than any other candidate in the race. Fully 84 percent of Clinton's coverage had been "negative in tone" compared to 43 percent for Trump and 17 percent for Sanders. The analysis was based on news statements by CBS, Fox, the *Los Angeles Times*, NBC, *The New York Times*, *USA Today*, *The Wall Street Journal*, and *The Washington Post*.

Key findings from January through June 2016 coverage included Trump received far more coverage than the other presidential candidates, positive in tone when the Republican race was still being contested and negative after the race had been decided. Although Sanders received "far less" coverage than Clinton, her coverage was "substantially more negative" than his. In addition, "the horserace" was the focus of reporting, rather than issues of character and policy or "fitness for the presidency" which received very little attention relative to the candidates' chances of winning (*Research: Media Coverage* 2016). Between the July through August 2016 post-convention period, Donald Trump received more press coverage than Hillary Clinton, but both candidates received negative coverage. Also, negative coverage of issue stands outpaced positive coverage 82 percent to 18 percent and, although Clinton's coverage was more positive than Trump's, it was still negative, with a tenth of her coverage revolving around "allegations of wrongdoing." Also, "context" was "largely missing from this negative coverage." To illustrate, although Clinton's emails were covered heavily by the media, relatively few stories provided the background—the harm caused by her actions and the degree to which other officials engaged in the same practice—which could have helped news audiences make sense of the issue (*Research: Media Coverage* 2016).

Finally, in the period from August through November 2016, including the general election, both Hillary Clinton and Donald Trump received "overwhelmingly negative coverage in tone and extremely light on policy." On topics relating to the candidates' "fitness for office," coverage was virtually identical in terms of its negative tone. In addition, political reporters generally "made no serious effort" to examine if "allegations surrounding Clinton" were "of the same order of magnitude as those surrounding Trump" (*Research: Media Coverage* 2016).

In 2006, *Washington Post* reporter Richard Cohen reflected on the massive and instantaneous and, on occasion, "verbal sewage" emailed feedback he had received in response to columns about Al Gore and Stephen Colbert:

> It seemed that most of my correspondents had been egged on to write me by various blogs. In response, they smartly assembled into a digital lynch mob and went roaring after me. If I did not like Colbert, I must like Bush. If I write for *The Post*, I must be a mainstream media warmonger. If I was over a certain age—which I am—I am simply out of it, whatever "it" may be. All in all, I was [am] the worthy object of ignorant, false and downright idiotic vituperation.

Cohen concluded that "the message in this case truly is the medium" in that the emails which "pulsed" in his queue emanated "raw hatred." This, he argued, indicated trouble ahead, not for the next GOP presidential candidate or Republicans in general, but for Democrats in that the anger "festering" on the "Democratic left" would eventually be taken out on the Democratic middle. Cohen's conclusion: "Watch out, Hillary" (2006).

This hypothetical from over a decade ago anticipated some of the media coverage of the 2016 presidential election. Billet (2016) believes that the explosion of digital mediation in contemporary political discourse has created for all candidates' individual personae or narratives which, regardless of truth, are "endlessly reproducible" through Twitter and Facebook. There has been a dominating narrative, particularly in the run-up to the primaries, made more exciting by an exaggerated, if not false, "David vs. Goliath" story about the Democrats. Sanders became the "David" in this narrative in that the press methodically and intentionally framed him as an outsider and anti-establishment alternative to Clinton's "Wicked Witch/career politician" persona so he would appear more "pristine" and even "innocent." In so doing, most of the media coverage ignored Sanders's actual and considerable "mainstream" political experience as evidenced by decades spent serving in Congress. While this exclusion resulted in Sanders being shielded from virtually any substantial negative press, Clinton (aka "Goliath") received more "issues coverage" than either Trump or Sanders. However, the more important point is that the vast majority of Clinton's coverage throughout the entire campaign cycle was far more negative than the stories "Tweeted and Facebooked" about either Bernie Sanders or Donald Trump (Capkronus 2016 and Childress 2016; see also Davis 2016).

SEVEN

Effects on the Electorate

It can be argued that factual knowledge about politics is a critical component of citizenship, essential if the public wants to discover significant interests and take advantage of the civic opportunities available to them. Hochschild (2010) maintains knowledge is the foundation to obtaining other responsibilities, without which neither "passion nor reason is likely to lead to decisions that reflect the real interests of the public." Some have argued that Donald Trump's dominance in the GOP primaries and, ultimately, in the November 8, 2016, presidential vote was both due to and a factor in the ignorance of his base of orphaned and polarized and uneducated Republicans. Their knowledge of current affairs was "too fractured" to recognize the extent to which his statements were false. As a result, his portion of the electorate was apparently not concerned that ignorance was a characteristic the Republican valued in his constituency, as indicated by statements such as "I love the poorly educated" (Stevenson 2016; see also Lowe 2016 and Camosy 2016). There is a paradox of American democracy and the prerequisites of democratic governance in that "every expansion of the franchise throughout American history has been understood to enhance democracy despite arguably reducing the politically relevant knowledge of the median voter" (Hochschild 2010).

However, Trump was telling the truth when he celebrated his Nevada caucus win with the tweet that he had won with not only the "lower educated" but the "highly educated" as well (Trump cited in Shepherd 2016). Trump generally enjoyed massive support from uneducated, low-information white voters. Hillary Clinton had a twenty-five percentage-point lead among college-educated voters going into the campaign. One *Foreign Policy* journalist observed the day after Donald Trump's November 2016 win that "never have educated voters so uniformly rejected a candidate" and "never before have the lesser-educated so uniformly supported a candidate." Trump supporters might have replied: "That's because Trump supports the little guy and Clinton helps the already privileged college grads." But that would have been false because his supporters in the primaries actually had an average income of about $72,000 per year, and made more than the national average and more than Clinton or Sanders supporters (Stevenson 2016).

Donald Trump may be obliged to the uninformed rather than the "under-educated" voter. Overall, American voters generally know who the president is but not much else. They believe the "system" is corrupt and rigged against them to benefit political elites on both sides of the aisle. For Republicans, this translates into a frustration that nothing happens and conservatives never make good on their promises. Democrats believe in problems of crony capitalism and the rise of income inequality on their watch.

DISTRUST OF DEMOCRATIC DIALOGUE

This frustration with the direction of the country and disdain for establishment politics has opened the door for outsider candidates such as Bernie Sanders and Donald Trump to dominate the campaign playing field like never before with appeals to their respective segments of the public. In addition, polarization has measurably increased in every aspect of American politics, from congressional voting to public opinion, with an especially dramatic rise in "negative partisanship"—distrust of and disdain for the other side (Krugman 2016a). While an easy place to lay blame, the celebrity status of candidates such as Donald Trump is not the only factor that catapults them to the top of their parties, despite lack of political experience or mainstream party affiliation. In Trump's case, the "experience deficit" may have "only made voters more willing" to accept him as a legitimate candidate for the presidency.

Affective Vulnerability

American populism as performed by Trump and expected by his base was rooted in the thought and culture of the country's "first populist president," Andrew Jackson. For Jacksonians—who formed the core of Trump's electorate—the United States is not a political entity created and defined by a set of intellectual propositions rooted in the Enlightenment and oriented toward the fulfillment of a universal mission. Instead, it is the nation-state of the American people, and its chief business lies at home with them and for them. The role of the government, therefore, is to fulfill the country's destiny by looking after their physical security and economic well-being and to do so "while interfering as little as possible with the individual freedom that makes the country unique" (Mead 2017).

What appears to be more lacking than usual in contemporary discourse is the balance of the "generous inclinations to see political controversy as rooted in reasonable or at least understandable disagreement, and to seek political reform through persuasive conversation and compromise." This may be due to the imbalance in the political process which

> leaves too little room for legislative deliberation, for experiences that would show each side that the other isn't driven mainly by callous indifference or irrational animosity. Another reason is the niche-y nature of our various media outlets, which allow people only to listen to commentators who reinforce their prejudices and fuel their self-righteousness (Peter Lawler quoted in Ross 2015).

Emotions are powerful to the extent that a significant portion of all decisions are based on affective factors—such as how one "feels" rather than what one "knows is right":

> [Voters] make decisions based on what [they] feel in the moment. Most Republican voters disagree with Trump's grotesque, lewd words on an intellectual level—but they still back the man because they feel defiant [and] that matters (Robbins 2016).

Flinders (2016) speaks of "the apparent rise in democratic disaffection." As president, Trump has continued to violate democratic norms and play to partisan emotion rather than consensus-building of any consequence—attacking judges, the media, and the legitimacy of the electoral process. In addition, even at an early point in his presidency, were his administration "to engage in outright authoritarian behavior," Donald Trump's default leadership style of polarization and division "has reduced the prospects that Congress would mobilize a bipartisan resistance or that the public would turn against him in masses" (Mickey, Levitsky, and Way 2017).

POLITICAL LITERACY AND THE ELECTORATE

Political information does influence how Americans vote. Every other year, the American National Election Studies surveys what voters know, what policies they support, and who they are (e.g., white or black, poor or rich, employed or not). The results of these surveys are that highly informed voters (regardless of income, ethnicity, gender, or party affiliation) tend to favor free trade and are pro-immigration. It is not just that a candidate's

> anti-trade and anti-immigrant agenda flies against the consensus of economists on the left, right, and center, but it's precisely the platform informed voters reject—regardless of their backgrounds. That's not to

say that high-information voters tend to favor the Democrats' politics. In fact, high-information voters tend to have policy preferences that cut across party lines. For instance, high-information voters are pro-free trade, pro-immigration, in favor of criminal justice reform, wish to raise taxes to offset the deficit, anti-war, pro-gay rights, and skeptical that the welfare state can solve all our problems (reported in Brennan 2016; see also *ANES Time Series Study* 2016).

Consequently, when policy platforms of the two major parties are examined, it becomes apparent that both the Republicans and Democrats push agendas that tend to appeal to the uninformed and disinterested. However,

We can't quite blame them for that. After all, politicians need to win elections, and to do so, they have to appeal to voters. In a modern democracy, the uninformed will always greatly outnumber the informed. The quality of our candidates reflects the quality of our electorate. But democracy encourages our electorate to be bad quality (Brennan 2016).

Party Convergence

This emerging pattern of enthusiasm followed by reality-induced disappointment and apathy on opposing sides of the aisle has been a major theme over the past few election cycles. Consequently, its impact on elections and the rise of Washington outsiders is important to the extent that there seems to be convergence in how Republican and Democratic voters select their elected officials. Such recurring patterns suggest that the American people as a whole share similar dissatisfaction with the political system and their choices in candidates. Trust in political institutions is an essential component of well-functioning democracies. Yet surveys by Pew, Gallup, and other polling agencies have confirmed that public confidence in government has slumped to historic lows in the United States. This has had a corrosive effect on the quality of democracy and created a "legitimacy crisis" (cited in Erickson 2017).

In addition, although it may be an easy answer to simply assert the American people are "just anti-establishment or anti-incumbent, that is not the message they are sending." The emerging dynamic demonstrates a rejection of the party establishments as well as of the overall political establishment in what appears to be an uncoordinated effort to purge government. Voters are not simply seeking the removal of deeply entrenched political leaders. They are revolting against the entire political industry and seeking elected officials who have not given in and will not succumb to Washington influences. They do not necessarily want bigger or smaller government; they want to overthrow the entire political class. In their voting choices, the electorate appears to be purging their government of entrenched political leaders, political money, special interests, dysfunctional bureaucrats, powerful technocrats, and all other parties that perpetuate the status quo of a government that no longer seems to serve them. Voters appear to be supporting candidates who they feel will confront these establishment groups instead of appeasing them (Geiger 2016).

MANDATE POLITICS

It may be tempting to assume that the United States' centuries-old democracy is impervious to democratic erosion, but such confidence is misplaced. Liberal democracy—with "full adult suffrage and broad protection of civil and political liberties"—is a relatively recent development in the United States. By contemporary standards, the country became fully democratic only in the 1970s (Mickey et al. 2017).

Evolving Partisanship

According to Chait (2015), the splitting of American politics into two coherent ideological parties with very little programmatic overlap changes the nation's public culture in that voters who are fundamentally attached to one party or the other are not going to easily abandon their party. While "some swing voters do still exist" and "performance can change voter perceptions to a degree,"

> these temporal effects are muted. The electorate is much less fluid than it used to be, and is more easily understood as hardened blocs defined by shared cultural identity (or shared mutual cultural antipathy) (Chait 2015).

Political polarization may be configured as a central factor behind democratic breakdown to the extent that extreme polarization could result in politicians and their supporters configuring their rivals as illegitimate and, in some cases, as "an existential threat" to the extent that democratic norms could

> weaken as politicians become willing to break the rules, cooperate with anti-democratic extremists, and even tolerate or encourage violence in order to keep their rivals out of power. Few democracies can survive for long under such conditions" (Mickey et al. 2017).

Williams (2014) identifies such politicians as belonging to "the new elite," a group comprised of "those who can shout loudest and more often" rather than those who can voice the most "cogent and most coherent response." Ultimately, such politicians coalesce to "foment a rabid culture of anti-rationalism where every fact is suspect; every shadow holds a secret conspiracy" with the result that "rational thought is the enemy" while "critical thinking is the devil's tool" (Williams 2014).

To illustrate, whether it was Donald Trump vowing to deport millions of undocumented immigrants, or Bernie Sanders promising a "political revolution," the campaign trail is "flooded with fantasies that will never, ever happen,"

> And yet the electorate seems hungry for those unrealistic and unachievable answers. More pies keep getting tossed into more skies—and more voters keep gobbling them up. . . . Governing is messy and complicated. It requires accommodation, not anger; determination, not delusion. But the overpromisers undermine that system and make compromise—the essence of democracy—much more difficult (Roberts and Roberts 2016b).

Cognitive Load

Chait (2015) suggests contemporary "voters form strong loyalties based more on loathing for the opposing party than on the old kind of tribal loyalty ('My daddy was a Democrat, his daddy was a Democrat. . . ') that used to prevail. The party system has split along racial, cultural, and religious lines, creating a kind of tribal system where each party's supporters regard the other side with incomprehension and loathing." Furthermore, strongly held beliefs about issues do not necessarily arise from "deep understanding" but rather from opinions which are reinforced by others, including political candidates and leaders (Kolbert 2017).

When voters are overwhelmed with false, or potentially false, statements, they experience "cognitive load." Eventually, without quite realizing it, "brains just give up trying to figure out what is true." While a strategy employed by the majority of American politicians, including Bernie Sanders and Hillary Clinton, Konnikova (2017) believes Donald Trump went further than others in the 2016 campaign in that he had a "particular untruth" he chose to propagate; his rhetoric was "not just an undifferentiated barrage" but he "simply" stated his opinion about whatever made him upset or angry "over and over" so that,

> As it turns out, sheer repetition of the same lie can eventually mark it as true in our heads. It's an effect known as illusory truth, first discovered in the '70s and most recently demonstrated with the rise of fake news.

Leda Cosmides at the University of California, Santa Barbara, points to her work with her colleague John Tooby on the use of a particular variation of this technique used to effectively mobilize voters during the 2016 campaign:

> The campaign was more about outrage than about policies . . . when a politician can create a sense of moral outrage, truth ceases to matter. People will go along with the emotion, support the cause and retrench

into their own core group identities. The actual substance stops being of any relevance (quoted in Konnikova 2017).

NEGOTIATING A POST-RHETORICAL PRESIDENCY

Vaughn (2016) maintains the United States is in the midst of a presidential post-rhetorical era, where "bully pulpit" leadership does not influence as much as it once did and unilateral presidential action, while increasingly common, is highly constrained and frequently ineffective. University of Texas professor Jeffrey Tulis argues that beginning with Woodrow Wilson and Theodore Roosevelt, American presidents began enacting a "rhetorical presidency" as they appealed directly to the electorate. They did so by taking advantage of mediated technologies in order to ostensibly engage a more fully realized democracy. However, as a result of the merging of this new doctrine of presidential power with an increasingly sophisticated mass media, and modifications in the presidential selection process, the constitutional balance between branches became destabilized (Stuckey 2016; see also Tulis 1987). And with the destabilization, "partisan polarization," perhaps the defining characteristic of contemporary American politics, emerged:

> Such is life in the post-rhetorical era, where party polarization, media saturation, and immunity to persuasion characterize the political environment in which presidents attempt, largely unsuccessfully, to lead. Presidential attempts to use what Theodore Roosevelt termed the bully pulpit almost always fail and presidential efforts to act alone prove unequal to the task. As the internet began to proliferate in the subsequent two decades, the nation developed a highly decentralized media system, one where today an individual essentially can find information sources that cater to their preferences regardless of where they fall on the ideological spectrum. The result today is an electorate that exists within an infinite number of echo chambers; unsurprisingly, the average Republican today is more conservative, the average Democrat is more liberal, the number of self-identified moderates continues to shrink, and the ideological distance between the median voter in each major party is greater than it has been in decades. . . . And yet a president today can't just throw [their] hands in the air and revert to a 20th Century vision of the office. Instead . . . they have adjusted in ways that are unique to the 21st Century (Vaughn 2016; see also Stuckey 2010, and Medhurst 2004).

THE DUNNING-KRUGER EFFECT

One such strategy of adjustment may be the emergence of the Dunning-Kruger Effect as a significant factor in determining the voting behavior of the contemporary American public. In sum, this cognitive perspective posits that "the knowledge and intelligence required to be good at a task are often the same qualities needed to recognize that one is not good at that task—and if one lacks such knowledge and intelligence, one remains ignorant that one is not good at that task" (Dunning 2016). Furthermore, this phenomenon holds over different domains of assessment, including logical reasoning, emotional intelligence, and political judgment. Similar deficiencies in insight have been found among poor chess players, unskilled medical lab technicians, medical students unsuccessfully completing an obstetrics/gynecology rotation, and people failing a test on performing CPR (Kruger and Dunning 1999).

Voter Misinformation or Electoral Ignorance

This misinformation problem can "live in" the public, as well. As an example, regardless of party affiliation, many voters frequently do not know which party controls Congress or what Congress has done recently or whether the economy is getting better or worse. In the 2000 U.S. presidential election, most voters knew Al Gore was more liberal than George W. Bush, but significantly less than half knew that Gore was more supportive of abortion rights, more supportive of welfare-state programs, favored a higher degree of aid to blacks, or was more supportive of environmental regulation (Madden 2015).

The reason for such behavior on the part of the electorate most likely has little if anything to do with "stupidity" or intellectual impairment. Somin (2013) suggests one of the most serious problems with modern democracy is that much of the public is usually ignorant of politics and government. This is primarily because of their contention that votes are unlikely to change the outcome of any election and so there is little reason to learn about politics. It may be that democracy as a system has "created bad incentives" and that the electorate remains misinformed because the costs to them of acquiring necessary information exceed the benefits of doing so:

> Most voters are ignorant or misinformed because the costs to them of acquiring political information greatly exceed the potential benefits. They can afford to indulge silly, false, delusional beliefs—precisely because such beliefs cost them nothing. After all, the chances that any individual vote will decide the election is vanishingly small. As a result, individual voters tend to vote expressively, to show their commitment to their worldview and team. Voting is more like doing the wave at a sports game than it is like choosing policy (Brennan 2016; see also Will 2014).

Yet, and perhaps ironically, while average Americans have incrementally become better educated over time, they have remained "equally ignorant about politics even as their education levels rose." In a different domain, such as political knowledge, one "focusing on intellectual rather than social abilities," the Dunning-Kruger Effect still holds:

> We chose logical reasoning, a skill central to the academic careers of the participants we tested and a skill that is called on frequently. We wondered if those who do poorly relative to their peers on a logical reasoning test would be unaware of their poor performance. . . . As expected, participants overestimated their logical reasoning ability relative to their peers (Kruger and Dunning 1999, 1124).

Attributing this phenomenon to an inept American education system is to misunderstand why citizens know so little. Public schools do teach most of what students need to know to vote well, much of which is forgotten because the information is not useful. This is because so many believe their individual votes make no difference. Furthermore, it has been suggested that encouraging citizens to "deliberate together" about politics "makes things worse, not better" and tends to reinforce partisanship and division (Brennan 2016). Writing in 2016, one of the original theorists commented about the relevance of the Dunning-Kruger Effect to contemporary politics:

> Essentially, they're not smart enough to realize they're "dumb" [in that] one's ignorance is completely invisible to them. [The key] is not that unknowledgeable voters are uninformed; it is that they are often misinformed—their heads filled with false data, facts and theories that can lead to misguided conclusions held with tenacious confidence and extreme partisanship, perhaps some that make them nod in agreement with Trump at his rallies. Trump himself also exemplifies this exact pattern, showing how the Dunning-Kruger Effect can lead to what seems an indomitable sense of certainty. All it takes is not knowing the point at which the proper application of a sensible idea turns into malpractice (Dunning 2016).

Poundstone (2017) suggests the Dunning-Kruger Effect is not a pathological condition but rather, is "the human condition." Accordingly, an individual may not have any doubt whatsoever about their ability to be Commander-in-Chief because that individual is afflicted, as all are on occasion, with "an incurable delusion of competence" (Poundstone 2017). Perhaps it may be a matter of degree as well as time and place that decides the severity of this "affliction." Regardless, in the case of the 2016 American presidential campaign, the problem becomes not that segments in the electorate or the particular candidates were too uninformed. It is that they did not know just how uninformed they were.

THE PARADOX PRESIDENT

A part of this unique enactment of a twenty-first-century post-rhetorical political environment might include what Texas A&M communication scholar Jennifer Mercieca calls "the rhetoric of demagoguery," used to describe the discourse of an American leader who "capitalizes on popular prejudices, makes false claims and promises, and uses arguments based on emotion rather than reason" (2015). Thus, it is unlikely that Chachi's appearance at the RNC yielded an electoral triumph for Donald Trump in November, just as Larry David's sense of Bernie Sanders probably did little to damage or enhance his prospects in the Democratic primary. Popular culture, nonetheless, serves the valuable and centrally important role of questioning and challenging; of asking voters to see politics and politicians differently. It does so by inviting new and different voices into the political dialogue and suggesting new and "provocative ways for citizens to reach the political judgments that are expected of them in a fully functioning, thriving democracy" (Parry-Giles 2016).

Contemporary voters may be misunderstanding two key elements of American democracy. The first is that elections matter and "so does electability" in that one cannot enact a program one cannot win. The second is that the political system was designed to distribute power, to slow down the process, to require negotiation and consensus rather than to polarize and provoke dissonance rather than consensus. It is, therefore, of concern when

> Candidates on both sides are also overpromising when it comes to [for example] replacing Supreme Court Justice Antonin Scalia. Most are outlining "litmus tests" and guaranteeing outcomes—an end to Obamacare, for example, or reversal of the Citizens United decision that demolished the campaign financing system. . . . The outbreak of overpromising didn't start this year. Tea Partiers told their followers that if they were elected to Congress, conservative canons would become law—a fanciful prospect that disregarded the basic power balance in Washington that they could not "wish away" (Roberts and Roberts, 2016b).

The Dunning-Kruger Effect may well be the key to the Trump voter and others—voters and politicians alike—and perhaps even to the man himself as he frequently evidenced significant gaps in crucial information necessary for the "job" of the presidency. While some have suggested his apparent ignorance of, for example, what a nuclear triad was or "decades" of U.S. foreign policy, were the result of narcissism and egotism. Brennan (2016) configures Donald Trump's campaign behavior "the other way around," suggesting that not seeing the mistakes for what they are "allows any potential narcissism and egotism to expand unchecked." In voters, lack of expertise would be unfortunate but perhaps not so concerning if the public had a concrete awareness of how imperfect their civic knowledge was. If they did, they could repair it. But the Dunning-Kruger Effect suggests something different: that some voters, especially those facing significant distress in their life, might like some of what they hear from their candidates, but "do not know enough to hold their candidates accountable for the serious gaffes they make or the untruths they share. This is because the voters fail to recognize those gaffes as missteps" (Dunning 2016) and the untruths as lies.

Voters who think they are informed may also be carrying a good deal of misinformation in their heads. In a survey conducted after the 2014 midterm elections, members of the electorate were asked whether they had voted. The key question was who was most likely to have voted: informed, uninformed, or misinformed citizens. Voting was strongly tied to whether those who took the survey thought of themselves as "well-informed" citizens. Perceiving oneself as informed was not necessarily tied to being well-informed. Furthermore, well-informed voters—whether "conservative or liberal"—accurately endorsed true statements about economic and social conditions in the United States—as long as those statements agreed with their politics. Conservatives truthfully claimed that the U.S. poverty rate had gone up during the Obama administration; liberals rightfully asserted that the unemployment rate had dropped.

It is significant that both groups also endorsed falsehoods agreeable to their politics. The "political lean" of the fact mattered more than its truth-value in determining whether respondents believed it. And endorsing partisan facts both true and false led to perceptions that one was an informed citizen, and then to a greater likelihood of voting. Given all this misinformation, confidently held, it is no wonder that a substantial portion of the exaggerations or untruths rhetorically presented during the 2016 presidential campaign caused so little outrage or scandal among those voters who found such candidates' views pleasing (Brennan 2016).

THE PARADOX-DEMOCRACY

A contributing factor in the evolution of the climate within which Bernie Sanders's and Donald Trump's divisive-partisanship discourse could thrive is "the paradox-democracy." This variation of American democracy has been described by Hochschild (2016) as a system which requires an informed electorate but is also "one in which enfranchising ill-informed citizens is a democratizing move" and therefore "has deep roots and wide applicability." Conversely, democracies thrive if citizens have some level of political knowledge and education associated with tolerance, civic engagement, and civil rights because each is "vital for prospective voting and preferable for retrospective voting." Regardless, Hochschild (2016) maintains that the benefits offered even if "only" by "the paradox-democracy" outweigh the costs in that:

> Obtaining the right to participate in democratic governance is a sign of respect, dignity, autonomy, and control for individuals and perhaps for the groups they represent; that is why so many people fought for so

long to ensure that women and African Americans could not participate.

There may be other virtues in this kind of democratic expansion as well,
including

> fear of social unrest if dissatisfied people have no legitimate channel to
> express grievances, provision of an arena to develop organizational
> capacities and promote civic virtue, and belief that each person is the
> best expositor of his or her own interests. [However] the point should
> be clear. Even if voters know too little to make choices that they would
> make with more knowledge, enabling them to participate creates a
> better government and better society than prohibiting them from doing
> so (Hochschild 2016).

Still, Lukianoff and Haidt (2015) assert that a healthy democracy "by
almost any definition," mandates "grounding one's beliefs in evidence
rather than in emotion or desire" and is dependent on "learning how to
search for and evaluate evidence that might contradict one's initial
hypothesis." Rather than assuming that "some democracy is better than
none at all," the Dunning-Kruger Effect informs an alternative and more
sobering vision. A possibility exists of a future within which, without
some kind of systemic intervention, a portion of the American electorate
will continue to consciously make political decisions which work against
even their own personal best interests as citizens of a constitutional democracy, the survival of which depends on their participation as a public
informed by critical thought and reflection.

EIGHT

The Post-Campaign Rhetorical Legacy

While extremist or fringe movements might emerge in other countries, initial conceptions of the 2016 American political culture, by contrast, were often framed as dominated by centrist figures like Jeb Bush and Hillary Clinton, much as in the past. It can be argued that a "politics of pessimism" has been one of the factors which has informed "fringe" or niche-focused American candidates like Donald Trump and Bernie Sanders, much as it did Marine Le Pen's rise in the National Front in France. Trump and Sanders's successes may evidence not only that Americans are losing their political faith but that contemporary politics is situated at some point on a "populist-to-fascist" continuum.

In theory, America has a government of the people, by the people, and for the people. In practice, Trump's and Sanders's joint and exceedingly effective message was that it has a government chosen by the people, to serve special interests, not their interests (Mahbubani 2016). The consensus of a 2017 Harvard Institute of Politics symposium, during which Kennedy School professors considered "whether or not modern democracy is threatened, "was in the affirmative. Reasons for their conclusion included Supreme Court campaign finance decisions; the marginalization of groups, including immigrants; the decline of political parties as well as civility in general; and the rise of populism (Ward 2017). Swanson (2017) maintains that one needs to "look no farther than the trio of President Donald Trump, Senator Bernie Sanders and Brexit" as evidence that populist-driven globalism is "both a wide-ranging and powerful force."

A POPULIST-TO-FASCIST CONTINUUM

Floyd Ciruli, director of the Crossley Center for Public Opinion Research at the University of Denver, identified four factors in American and European democracies that lead to the divisive rhetoric and the trend toward revolutionary change that has characterized this election season. These are first, economic distress, which creates class divisions that force voters to seek out fringe candidates they feel will better represent their interests than "elite" politicians and bureaucracies. Second, demographic trends, including the current leaning of the millennial generation away from traditional institutions and values and toward broad, sweeping change that requires more passion than it does experience. Third, global displacement, reflecting conflicts throughout the world that lead people to seek security in Western countries, where existing populations and the pressure to assimilate continue to cause tension. And finally, concerns about national security, which rest on the existence of global displacement and violent conflict, shift voters toward increased domestic security and a bolder stance on foreign policy (Ciruli 2016).

Globalism has become imbalanced because specific groups are benefitting in extraordinary ways at the expense of other groups. The challenge is not to reverse or oppose globalization but to configure or rebalance it in a way that will provide broad gains to those "outsiders" (aka "orphaned electorates") who feel they have been excluded. Right-wing populism (e.g., Brexit and Trump's campaign) thrives in such an environment because it has no stake in either liberal democracy or a liberal world economy. Left-wing populism emerges within a different environment, but both default to similar discourses. For example, Bernie Sanders and Donald Trump both shared "an angry tone and a raw, un-politician-like affect" which their supporters found authentic and persuasive. This enabled them to orchestrate campaigns driven by waves of populist support maintained through their supporters' anger against the status quo (Dickinson 2015).

POPULISM

Swanson (2017) suggests that while left-wing populism falls along economic divides, right-wing populism is a response to ethnic and national differences. It is distinguished from left-wing populism (e.g., Sanders's campaign) in that the latter at least offers remedies that might address and even eliminate the divisions which create the backlash in the first place. Such populists talk about inequality of opportunity and income and wealth, and at times suggest solutions to remedy the imbalances. Conversely, right-wing populism (e.g., Trump's campaign) is sustained by cultural, ethnic, racial, and religious fractures that are intentionally exacerbated to make it successful (see Zakaria 2016). In other words, right-wing populists actively create an enemy that can mobilize their supporters. As such, they are more dangerous than their left-leaning contemporaries, because their remedies entail deepening the fractures they have created and on which they thrive.

In addition, right-wing populists generally have little need or respect for the norms of liberal democracy because they believe that there is one true national will or state or country. As such, they generally abhor and even mock concepts such as pluralism or multi-culturalism and, in some cases, institutions like a free independent judiciary. As a result, populism may be differently framed, as a right-wing, ethno-nationalistic, racialist narrative, or a left-wing social and economic exclusion narrative. As an example, the massive influx and movement of refugees into Western Europe, which has been globally monitored, equated with terrorism and extensively covered daily by traditional and digital media, including that in the United States, makes it easier for right-wing than left-wing organizations to win converts organizing this broad-based discontent. In sum, moving forward, "right-wing populism is likely more dangerous to democracy than left-wing populism":

> [There is] a distinction between the deep causes of populism and the political narratives around which they get wrapped. The deep causes of populism are economic and structural, generally speaking. There might be residues of racism and ethno-nationalism in the United States and other European countries, but [that's not] what's really driving populism. What's driving it is the economic insecurities, the rising inequality and the economic and social divisions that have been created, not just by globalization, but by the kind of policies we have pursued in the last few decades (Swanson 2017).

Divisive Unification

However, the divisive partisanship campaigns of both Sanders and Trump contributed to an unstable and essentially unprecedented enactment of the United States' constitutional democracy. In contrast to their twentieth-century contemporaries, Azari (2014) believes that twenty-first century American presidents function within a culture of constant "mandate politics" in that they "draw on the logic of campaign promises and election results much more frequently." The era of mandate politics has been building for decades, starting with Richard Nixon's appeals to a "silent majority" and Ronald Reagan's case for a "conservative mandate" to the "will of the electorate" candidacies and presidencies of George W. Bush and Barack Obama. The "content" of "mandate rhetoric" has also changed with election results being tied to specific policies rather than broader ideas about national or party values" (Azari 2014, 2).

While early populists "wove threads of nativism and xenophobia" into their rhetoric, their primary targets were the "elites of their time," monopolies, banks, and industrialists, and economic barons on whom politicians blamed the troubles of "little people"—albeit most often white

Christian "little people" —for their loss of livelihood and status. Originally identified as an attribute of right-oriented political parties, since the
ideological in party orientation and the "disruption" of their relevance,
populism is now present in the political discourse of parties "attempting
to achieve their goals regardless of their ideological orientation or heritage." In this sense, populism is a "new-old means" for

> the conquest of hearts of the people by those political parties in govern-
> ment or opposition that may be left, right or central oriented [trans-
> forming] from an ideological label toward a means for massive win-
> ning of votes and support for candidates in the political campaign-
> ing . . . conducted with uninterrupted rhetoric through the entire peri-
> od of political activity and not only in front of election. Especially with
> the enormous growth of the use of social networks in the political
> campaigning [it] is finding its way [into] the discourse of political ac-
> tors . . . and transforming itself into a fast-track way to come to power
> via practicing the symbolic politics (Latifi 2015).

Furthermore, both left- and right-wing parties in such populist contexts
generally do not rely on the development of political options for their
parties. Instead, they engage in a rhetoric of personal blame, threats, and
improvisations of frequently empty projects rather than discourse about
issues which are relevant to their publics (see Wodak 2015).

In Steinhorn's (2017) view, the "magic behind Donald Trump's 2016
campaign" populist success was that he promised his segment of the
"orphaned electorate" that the only way to "make America great again"
was by restoring their status as the ones who made America great in the
first place—which "is exactly how they see themselves." In this view,
Trump's base of white working-class Americans was a "constituency
ripe" for his rhetoric:

> They were the real heroes of post-World War II America, the ones who
> made our prosperity and pre-eminence possible. Theirs is a narrative of
> an American century built by smokestack industries and sturdy white
> men with a blue-collar, lunch-pail ethic that would come to define the
> middle class of the post-war years. . . . That they may have benefited
> from the racial and gender discrimination of those years is immaterial
> to how they saw themselves. They played by the rules and they earned
> it (Steinhorn 2017).

When their jobs began to disappear, these men also lost the prestige
which accompanied membership in the working class. The twenty-first-
century post-industrial American knowledge economy "celebrate[s]
brains, over brawn, the creative class over the working class, the . . . geek
who constructs algorithms over the hard hat" (Steinhorn 2017). All but
ignored by mainstream politicians, a fully developed populism emerged
in Campaign 2016 delivered through the campaigns of Bernie Sanders
and Donald Trump, but with noticeable differences.

Sanders's and Trump's Populism

Bernie Sanders's populism, with its dominant theme of anti-corporatism targeting his primarily white, college-educated, decidedly unhappy—if not overtly angry—disenfranchised base, was a throwback to earlier populist discourses. While his "one with the people" talk targeting party elites and wealthy special-interest groups may have endeared him to his base, his self-identification as a socialist combined with his "populist forays" against Wall Street allowed Sanders to reach beyond that base (Chait 2016). Sanders's strength as a populist candidate was the symbolism of his self-pronounced "outsider" status rather than a particular stand on issues (Woodruff 2016). Before he was declared the winner of the Indiana primary, Sanders spoke to 7,000 followers at a Kentucky rally during which he hit off his major populist themes like health care reform, Social Security, immigration, and the U.S. criminal justice system with "some of the evening's biggest cheers" coming after he called for raising the minimum wage to $15 an hour. Sanders also drew strong support by calling for gender pay equity. He also spoke of ending the "embarrassment of women" making 79 cents on the dollar compared to men; insisted "we need the best workforce in the world;" reiterated his call for free tuition for public colleges and universities, saying "we need the best-educated workforce in the world"; insisted "now is the time for Wall Street to help the middle class of this country," and demanded a "revolution in mental health treatment" (quoted in Kazin 2016).

Conversely, Donald Trump's pre-election populist rhetoric was grounded in raw pathos, created to inflame a white working-class with a palpable and personalized anger at those his "forgotten Americans" needed to believe deprived them of their cultural capital. Trump understood all of that from the very beginning of his campaign. Sporting his trademark "Make America Great Again" red baseball cap signaling white working-class solidarity, he vowed to stomp on the elites that his supporters believed were putting them down. He may have promised them a return of their manufacturing jobs, but he did so with "a wink and a nod" as both he and they knew that these jobs weren't "really coming back." Instead, the real vindication he offered was a cultural revival and a supersized serving of respect—as well as the satisfaction of "sticking it to their politically correct, patronizing foes."

One irony of the most recent national elections in the United States, is that appealing to traditional American democratic values (e.g., those of "mainstream politicians") may fail to energize a base of voters who do not understand, value, or accept said values. In such cases, it might pay for a candidate to distance her/himself from at least some of the values of the constitutional democracy in order to get elected. While governing may be the "art of compromise" a candidate who wants to win an election, might support voter's demands, regardless of whether or not those demands facilitate democratic values such as "equal respect" or inclusion:

> What we are seeing in both Congress and the presidential campaign is a yearning for politicians who reject commitment to . . . our democracy. Since [such] candidates who reject [for example] equal respect win office by explicitly flouting democratic values, there is no reason to think that, once in office, they will suddenly embrace them. There is no reason to think that any democratic values, such as free and fair elections, will be safe from them. We can expect such politicians to engage in undemocratic practices . . . all in the service of protecting the perspectives of their voters (Stanley 2015).

SANDERS'S AND TRUMP'S DEMAGOGIC APPEALS

Both outsider candidates were labeled as demagogues, with Sanders enacting his version as an "inane socialist" and Trump performing his version as a "foul-mouthed nationalist" (Charen 2016). Somin (2016) suggests that, together, Sanders and Trump used demagogic devices which included exploiting ignorance regarding trade issues in their orphaned bases. Like Donald Trump, Bernie Sanders put forward budget projections that experts, even in their own parties, regarded as "fantastical." As a result, their disenfranchised and ill-formed segments of the electorate agreed with Trump's and Sanders's joint claim that the country could only deal with "our" serious fiscal problems by massive reforms but also massive spending increases (Sanders) and massive tax cuts (Trump). In addition, both situated their campaign discourses to exploit the fragility and vulnerabilities of the country's late-democratic system, which included "hyperdemocratic" messages (Sullivan 2016). Together, they were "dangerous men" who "just say what people want to hear and never explain how they're going to do it":

> They try to adhere to the sentiment of the masses and use those emotions as their sole justification. Both try to demean a class of people that are the most hated in our country so they can make themselves look like the "people's leader," trying to fight against the bad guys. [Both] are radicals, with extravagant claims which hold no logical backing (Borosage 2015).

Bernie Sanders may have been a "demagogue of the left," evidenced by rhetorical behaviors which included harsh and repetitive criticisms of Hillary Clinton's expertise and experience as merely more evidence that American democracy was in grave trouble and needed a complete "do over," which only a "Bernie Revolution" could accomplish. Donald Trump may also have been a demagogue, evidenced by rhetorical behavior grounded in a "tyrannical character plucked directly out of [Plato's "Republic"] one of the first books about politics ever written" (Sullivan

2016). Still, on a populist-to-fascist continuum, Bernie Sanders would most likely be situated on one end of the spectrum as a fully engaged and engaging populist while Donald Trump would occupy the opposite end, as demagogic and possibly proto-fascist. Both exploited a divided country. On the right, this meant proposals to crack down on immigrants, Muslims, and outsiders of all kinds. On the left, it meant demands to downsize big banks, crack down on tax-dodging multinationals, shift to a much more progressive tax system, and get serious about curbing carbon emissions. Cassidy (2016) suggests Sanders particularly embraced a "left-leaning" populism with his demands for a "political revolution," attacks against the "billionaire class," and embracing the label "democratic socialist," language that had never been heard before in a Democratic presidential primary (see also Kazin 2016).

POPULAR AND MOB DEMOCRACY

Nevius (2016) believes the 2016 presidential campaign revealed a future for American politics informed by "pure demagoguery, with candidates like Trump who can say whatever plays best in the moment and never be taken to task for it." For example, in discussions of government debt, Trump first proposed the "potentially disastrous policy" that the United States renegotiate its debt payments with foreign creditors. Almost immediately, he walked that back, instead remarking: "I said if we can buy back government debt at a discount—in other words if interest rates go up and we can buy bonds back at a discount—if we are liquid enough as a country, we should do that" (quoted in Nevius 2016).

Informed Electorate vs. Mob Democracy

Burke's concepts of "identification" and "division" provide a prescriptive social vocabulary concerned with the "health" of the electorate's interpretations as evidenced in their relationships with others. Thus, the goal of identification and division in the context of politicians and their constituencies is not reduced to matters of expediency, but to "the proper governance of the self-acting in society" (White 2003). Inadequate voter knowledge prevents government from reflecting the will of the people in any meaningful way. Such ignorance also raises doubts about democracy as a means of serving the interests of a majority.

Somin (2004) argues the American electorate does not have adequate knowledge for voters to control public policy. Scholars have long documented the limits of voter knowledge about the institutions and policies of the government. That ignorance is not a moral failing. The rational voter has little incentive to gain more knowledge about politics because his or her vote is unlikely to affect the outcome. Since gaining more knowledge offers few benefits and substantial costs, the average citizen remains ignorant, though rationally so. Some scholars have argued that citizens use "shortcuts" to gain enough knowledge to participate in self-government. The evidence does not support the "shortcut" argument.

It is a valid point, however, to recognize that the size of modern government is often so great that it is impossible for voters—even the most knowledgeable among them—to be adequately informed about its operations. Smaller government may actually be more easily democratic than the form of democracy presently enacted in the United States: voters would be more likely to exercise informed control over policy. Still, voter ignorance also suggests the value of decentralized federalism. In a decentralized federal system, citizens may "vote with their feet" by moving out of jurisdictions with policies they dislike and into those that have more favorable ones. Because each person decides whether or not to move, there is a much greater incentive to acquire relevant information with "foot voting" than with traditional voting at the polls (Somin 2004).

IMPLICATIONS

Eighteenth-century Americans feared demagogues, whose inflammatory rhetoric "stirred the very passions that the Founders hoped to control," which Andrew Trees, a Carthage College adjunct history professor suggested in March 2016 may be an "apt description of Trump's campaign":

> Many of the checks and balances in the Constitution were put there precisely so that people like Trump would not be able to win an election . . . the Founders feared men such as Patrick Henry, with his impassioned and persuasive oratory. . . . The role of political parties . . . complicates matters . . . but would not have changed [their] overall view [as they] almost universally hated political parties and were distressed when the new republic quickly gave rise to protoparties (true political parties . . . did not exist until well into the 19th century) . . . the problem with a political party was that it went directly against the kind of dispassionate reason they hoped would guide all political debates by requiring men to hew the party line, regardless of their conscience (Trees 2016).

To that end, the Founders would most likely have praised party leadership who undermined "their own nominating process to keep a man such as Trump from winning" because of "doing what wise statesmen are supposed to do—dampening the passion and allowing reason to rule" (Trees 2016).

It can also be argued that Americans lack a vocabulary to describe the behavior of political crowds which become inflamed with "populist passion" and become "citizens in the mass" who act "as tyrannical as any king" (John Adams quoted in Traub 2016). And while "to believe in democracy is to embrace the crowd," it may be as equally a valid assumption that:

> At moments of great division, the mob can be summoned by a figure who exploits its anger and fear. Europeans, with their long tradition of populist fascism, know this far better than Americans, who nevertheless have had their own populist rabble-rousers— Father Coughlin, Huey Long, George C. Wallace, Patrick J. Buchanan (Traub 2016).

Donald Trump, channeled through digitally mediated rhetoric, may be a twenty-first-century "impresario of the mob"—an instrument of the crowd who feels its resentment, its impatience, its distrust, and returns them all in slogans, epithets, and taunts. He validated his "orphaned" Americans' malice by speaking out loud things people are not sure they have a right to say: "torture the terrorists, kick out the immigrants" (Traub 2016). Ultimately, this rhetorically created differentiation split marginalized voters from the Democratic and Republican mainstream and each other to the extent that:

> Insults and sparring reached a fevered pitch on the Republican side of the race that the Democratic candidates have not matched. . . . Republican voters are far more likely to view the race as divisive (Foran 2016b).

Trump discursively situated his marginalized conservative-right electorate as outsiders, abandoned by mainstream politicians, in need of saving (by him) from further assaults by "her" (Hillary Clinton).

Philosopher Hannah Arendt wrote about the "banality of evil" and how people rationalize themselves as "just doing their job," yet become complicit in acts of murder (1963). Arendt also describes those who thought that Hitler's rise was a terrible thing but chose "internal exile," or staying invisible and out of the way as their strategy for coping with the situation. They knew evil was evil, but they too facilitated it, by departing from the battlefield out of a sense of hopelessness (Arendt 1968). Allen (2016) argues both of these phenomena have occurred during the 2016 presidential race, particularly evidenced in the campaign of Donald Trump, a "rabble rouser" who had "found his rabble" (Traub 2016). The first showed itself, for instance, when journalists covered every crude and cruel statement as "just doing their jobs" while the second is experienced in "mundane" everyday conversations which culminate in silence, frustration, a sense of impotence. But Trump's campaign moved beyond Arendt's concerns in that he exploited the inability of most Americans to unite across ideological divides and, despite being a "candidate with significant weaknesses" which his "party knew quite well" resulted in a head-to-head contest against Clinton (Allen 2016). The result was the "perfect storm" of conditions which produced what, up to and including the early morning hours of November 9, 2016, had been unimaginable.

New York Times columnist Charles Blow (2016a) considers Donald Trump to be more than a populist, not only "nativist and sexist" but also a "disarming and terrifyingly dangerous" man, a "fascist and racist demagogue" who twisted the truth as the front-runner in the race to become the Republican Party's presidential nominee (see also Keane 2016). Roger Cohen (2016) argued that the United States was "ripe for Trump just as Italy was ripe for Berlusconi":

> Trump, too, is cutting through a rotten political system in a society where economic frustration at jobs exported to China is high. He is emerging from two lost wars, as American power declines and others strut the global stage, against a backdrop of partisan political paralysis, in a system corrupted by money. To Obama's Doctrine of Restraint, Trump opposes a Doctrine of Resurgence. To reason, he counters with rage.

The "outsider" divisive discourse of Sanders as well as that of Trump appealed to voters fundamentally attracted to campaign promises that preferenced, expanded, and protected their own interests over those which embraced traditional democratic values. This became an organic component of both campaigns because "people tend to take out their resentment on groups they believe don't share their way of life" (Stanley 2015). Ultimately, this strategy of engendering populist division in voters evolved into a continually reinforced anger and sense of abandonment by each candidate. By rhetorically exaggerating the perceptions that no other candidates shared their constituents' "way of life" or understood their sense of betrayal by "mainstream" politicians, Sanders's and Trump's populist rhetoric of divisive partisanship may have, intentionally or not, moved the United States further along the "populist-to-fascist" continuum.

.

Global Default Discourses

America's political system, where anger is the tone and a lack of experience is increasingly a valued characteristic, is not alone in experiencing the "seismic tremor" of protofascist (see Kelley 2007) discourse. Floyd Ciruli, director for the Crossley Center for Public Opinion Research at the University of Denver, contends similar turmoil is visible in Europe as formerly marginalized parties and leaders gain traction (2016). Angry and disenfranchised nationalists and populists won by running against the European Union and many of its member states' establishments, further driven by the immigration crisis. And while frustration with the European establishment shows signs of gaining momentum, a host of polling indicators in the U.S. has been flashing red for a decade. Public satisfaction with Washington at the end of the Bush era fell below thirty percent, nearly matching the president's final approval rating of thirty-five percent.

Although Barack Obama started with extremely positive approval ratings, his first summer brought the newly formed Tea Party out in force, and Democrats started losing Senate, congressional, and gubernatorial elections. By 2016, they were at the lowest point of influence since World War II while Obama's approval rating seldom climbed to fifty percent. In addition, only one-quarter of the population believed the country is going in the "right direction," and approval of Congress was in the teens. Ciruli (2016) also observes that, periodically, an outsider shakes up America's dominant parties. Barry Goldwater with the Republicans in 1964 and George McGovern with the Democrats in 1972 took control of their respective parties and proceeded to lose in landslides. Still, by 2016, the level and length of the turmoil was considered unprecedented, setting the stage for either party to pick an outsider, ultimately condemning "establishment" candidates on both sides of the aisle to suffer a substantial defeat, which ultimately proved to be the case.

In this view, several factors drove and continue to fuel the angry rhetoric and radical change in the United States as well as in European democracies. These include economic distress, demographic trends, global displacement, and national security. Ciruli's (2016) words, written before Trump's win, proved both prophetic and problematic:

> It's not clear whether the anger of voters will energize productive change or threaten democracy, but in 2016, hot rhetoric and various combinations of nationalism, populism and nativism are so far proving very fruitful for the outsider (see also Kelemen 2016).

FASCISM AS EXTREME POPULISM

While the examination of whether or not fascism, as a form of government and social organization, has emerged as a political system in the United States is beyond the scope of the current study, it is nonetheless a topic to consider, albeit briefly. As a child growing up in World War II Italy, Umberto Eco experienced fascism directly. A half-century later, he was concerned that such leadership could again appear in the world and grow into various political regimes, driven by charismatic leaders who reject democracy through openly embracing populist appeals informed by factors including corporatism, imperialism, and nationalism. Maintaining that "the fascist game can be played in many forms," Eco nonetheless believed that its basic tenets could be understood as "a way of thinking and feeling, a group of cultural habits, of obscure instinct" outlined as a list of features that were typical of what he called "Ur-Fascism, or Eternal Fascism" (1995).

Briefly, these features include a "cult of tradition" which guarantees that "truth has been spelled out once and for all"; a rejection of modernism in favor of irrationalism, and a basic distrust of the "intellectual world" to the extent that "thinking is a form of emasculation." Other features of "Ur-Fascism" include the framing of disagreement as treason rather than as a way to improve knowledge and exploiting a "fear of difference" which results in behavior such as racism to "appeal against intruders." In addition, Ur-Fascism panders to a "frustrated middle class" which suffers from economic crisis or feelings of "political humiliation" and fear of lower social groups. It also privileges "being born in the same country" as the defining feature of social identity; strives to make "followers" humiliated by anyone who has more "wealth" than they do, combined with creating a sense that followers can completely "overwhelm" their "enemies."

Pacifism is configured as "trafficking with the enemy" since life is "permanent warfare against enemies" who want to control the world while a "popular elitism" is mandated, which guarantees "every citizen belongs to the best people in the world." This combines with leadership whose power is not democratically derived and who consider the "masses" so weak as to "need and deserve a ruler." Heroism becomes a "norm" with "heroic death" imagined as the "best reward for a heroic life" so that the "Ur-Fascist hero" frequently "sends other people to death." "Machismo"—characterized by both "disdain for women" and condemnation of "nonstandard sexual habits"—is privileged and supporters tend to "play with weapons" as substitutions for sex, "a difficult game to play." Finally, Ur-Fascists communicate through "Newspeak," which foregrounds characteristics such as an "impoverished vocabulary" and an "elementary syntax" in order to "limit the instruments for complex and critical reasoning" (Eco 1995).

Certainly, there are aspects of Eco's framework in the way many popular American politicians talk. However, Donald Trump's style in particular, including his conservative populism from angry rhetoric on immigrants and global trade to his default choice of Twitter for disseminating messages, has provoked a discussion about the possibility of fascism developing in the United States through his leadership. Some have insisted that Trump does not make it easy to refrain from calling him a fascist (see Paxton 1998; Rohac and Zilinsky 2015; Savel 2016; McNeill 2016).

Billet (2016) maintains that, more than any other American presidential candidate in recent memory, Donald Trump understood the ideological power, "the raw manipulative magic," in politics as aesthetics. Cultural theorist Walter Benjamin (1936) expressed great concern regarding the advent of reproductive technologies that were making works of art universally accessible to the public in a way that had never before been possible. A "fascist" would use such "easy access" not to respect people's access to such information as "their right" but instead "as a chance to express themselves." Benjamin argued the ability to reproduce an image or a sound countless times created the potential for the democratization of art. However, that democratization was prevented by the means for that reproduction remaining in the hands of a few. As such, it was possible for undemocratic regimes and governments to use art for their own benefit in ways previously considered impossible. Billet argues Benjamin was clearly writing about Nazi Germany:

> . . . a regime that knew how to deploy aesthetics ingeniously. Even as Hitler and the Third Reich railed against the poisons of modernity, they both used the latest technology to relay their message. They grabbed people's attention and held it, igniting their imaginations and providing them with a sense of ownership over a system that would just as soon see them driven into dirt (2016).

In this interpretation, Nazi fascism sought to give "the people" an expression while preserving property so that its logical result was the introduction of aesthetics into political life:

> The crisp, angular uniforms for party members cranked out by the thousands, the massive orchestrated rallies, the technologically innovative films of Leni Riefenstahl—these are all perfect examples of how fascism aestheticized politics to its own end. All employed the rhythmic regimentation of life, the fetishization of raw power and sacrifice for the Fatherland. Violence was not celebrated for its own sake, but was seen as a necessary and fascinating virtue, even beautiful for its ability to mobilize people's minds and bodies (Billet 2016).

Pottle (1999) argues Benjamin's vision of a world saturated with artistic images has been realized to a degree that might well have exceeded his wildest expectations. Multimedia technology is affecting human's perception of reality, "divorcing our definition of authenticity from its former prerequisite of physical existence"—but to what means? Are humans moving toward "the art of a classless society," or does the mass-mediated and hyper-texted dissemination of images result in a "a processing of data in the Fascist sense?" Furthermore, the questions and concerns regarding the social consequences of such proliferation in the twenty-first century are uniquely significant, particularly in light of Donald Trump's mediated campaign and political ascendency:

> Postmodern cultural logic has made meaning and coherence flexible, relative, accountable not to facts, but to subjective feelings [so that] the aestheticization of politics is more effortless than ever. . . . Social media has made the individual persona or narrative, regardless of truth, endlessly reproducible through the electronic channels of Twitter and Facebook. Trump clearly knows this. And his time on *The Apprentice* proved that his *Lifestyles of the Rich and Famous* manner was ultimately adaptable to a 21st-century cultural tenor. He has a bottomless bank account to back it up. Add in a white, increasingly old middle

class, palpably anxious about whether their days are numbered that can seal themselves in a media bubble echo chamber should they really want to, and you've gone a long way toward explaining what's underneath Trump's poll numbers—and what makes him somewhat exceptional. . . . His media strategists are masters at detaching meaning from fact, making words accountable only to themselves and how loudly they're shrieked. This makes him a quintessentially postmodern candidate contrasted to an age when the cold, everyday facts of collapse, crisis and apocalypse are unavoidable (Billet 2016).

Blow (2016c) cautions against imagining that a vigorous American "Trump-Sanders" coalition, let alone fascist movement, could ever exist in that Trump's supporters saw "a country in decline, a government . . . out of control and incompetent, an influx of immigrants that represent an existential threat and a culture that is hamstrung by political correctness." Conversely, Sanders's base saw a democracy disappearing into oligarchy. For them, the United States was a country that had

> . . . utterly failed to keep pace with is global peers on social structure issues—and economic equality taxation, health care and education [and had] gone . . . off the rails on many others, like criminal justice and mass incarceration.

Also, when comparing Trump's leadership to the fractious politics of most European countries—either historically or currently—Americans actually have a narrow range of political opinions, steeped in a broad political consensus on the legitimacy of democracy, free enterprise, and individual liberties. In addition, the United States has never shown itself to be susceptible to the kind of far right or left movements that rose to power in Europe in the twentieth century (Marchant 2016). Taub (2016) states that the GOP, by positioning itself as the party of traditional values and law and order, has attracted what was previously a large bipartisan population of Americans with authoritarian tendencies. Trump's "simple, powerful, and punitive" style could be the embodiment of a leader that would appeal to such a base. And while it does appear that Donald Trump often and with substantial success taps into a vein of very real fear, and uses "virtually any unmoored fact" he can find to mobilize it, "it is quite incorrect to label his right-wing populism as fascist" although, in the future:

> It is not impossible that [Trump] could pull a Father Coughlin. That there are open white supremacists campaigning for him shows that the raw materials are there, waiting to be pieced together. That his campaign is able to employ an "aesthetic strategy"—though they would likely never acknowledge it—reveals an ability to do so. (Billet 2016).

Some have suggested it is troublesome to even suggest that Trump could be a fascist. To spotlight this concern, there is the success of Bernie Sanders, a self-declared but mislabeled "democratic socialist," in the 2016

Democratic primary and his continuing influence due in part to this mis-perception, despite his loss to Hillary Clinton. While voters old enough to remember the Cold War might find the "socialist" label off-putting, younger voters to whom Sanders appealed may have a different associa-tion. "For seven years, they've heard Barack Obama called a socialist. So they think, 'if that's socialism, it's not that bad.'" (Marchant 2016). As such, if so many Americans can actually, albeit mistakenly, come to be-lieve Bernie Sanders is a socialist, it is just as likely that mislabeling Donald Trump as fascist, even though he is not, may help to soften the word and thus make it easier for a something closer to "real fascism" which existed in Europe to arise on American soil in the future (Marchant 2016).

INTERVENTION OPTIONS

Regardless of where Bernie Sanders and Donald Trump, respectively, may fall on a "populist-to-fascist" continuum, it is still telling that each in his own way tapped into at least some of the aforementioned discursive behaviors as they enacted campaigns of divisive partisanship. Eco ac-knowledged that the features of Ur Fascism could not easily be organized into a system in that several of them contradict each other, and could be symptomatic of other types of despotism or fanaticism. Yet, he also in-sisted "it is enough that one of them be present to allow fascism to coagu-late around it" (1995). To that end, while attempts to draw such a connec-tion may be "tangled up with Internet memes," it may be more "intellec-tually honest" to argue that Bernie Sanders and Donald Trump, as they planned and executed their campaigns of divisive partisan rhetoric, em-ployed at least some of the elements of fascism identified by Eco, who "had lived through Italian fascism" and who understood "that words, even the most banal, have meaning" (Berry 2016).

One possibility to countering the populist-to-fascist trend in the West, including that represented by the Trump/Sanders campaign perfor-mances in 2016, includes the countering of dominant negative mediated narratives with positive and more accurate narratives. In this way, the story of Western civilization and, in particular, democratic nations "go-ing off the rails" becomes re-constituted to reflect the reality that, objec-tively speaking, the world is not being derailed. Mediated stories for publics would then reflect—and so provide information about—fairer representations of Western democracies including that military conflicts are on a long-term declining trend; poverty is diminishing; middle-class populations are "exploding all around the globe"; new markets are emerging and that, with the right leadership, Western countries, like the rest, can hope for better futures (Mahbubani 2016).

NINE

Implications of Divisive Partisanship Rhetoric

There were multiple contributing factors which coalesced into the "perfect storm" which produced Hillary Clinton's November 2016 loss to Donald Trump. The entire campaign had been informed by the global wave of populist discontent with the status quo that had been signaled earlier in the year by the British "Brexit" vote, which Kakutani (2017) believes helped fuel the rise of both Sanders and Trump. Other mitigating circumstances included "the foibles of the candidate herself" (Halpern 2017), whose campaign has been described as being "as rigid and empty as it was when she lost in 2008." Clinton was hampered as well by her decision to give paid speeches to investment banks, that her campaign managers "took their eyes off the ball," and that she was a "policy wonk" (Troy 2016; see also Long 2016; M. Weiss 2016, and Montanaro 2016). In Gitlin's (2017) view she "contributed to her own defeat" orchestrated by an "inner core of campaigners" who were "tone-deaf" as to what the electorate was feeling. Clinton's operations were "in the hands of clueless number-crunchers." And, "most damagingly," she failed to construct a "big programmatic message" by tapping into the same "gross angers" as Trump.

Sexism has also been factored in as a possible contributing reason for Clinton's inability to win the presidency, to the extent that one reporter early in the campaign requested that women readers, whether "Bernie" or "Hillary" supporters, "think about the straight white men in your life" and ask if "you personally know even one straight white man backing Clinton in this election" (Bohanan 2016: see also Cottle 2016). In Klein's (2017) opinion:

> Many of Clinton's strengths were hidden by our gendered expectations of leaders—what she was good at would have been important for her presidency, but it is not what 44 male presidents in a row have taught us to expect, or even to see.

Healy (2016a) reports that white males consistently indicated their preference for either Donald Trump or Bernie Sanders to a "potential female president" during the 2016 presidential campaign, while Bump (2016c) believes that Clinton's most serious campaign "relationship problem" was with white men, on policy issues as well as stylistically (Bump 2016c; see also Bordo 2017). Cottle (2016) maintains "raw political sexism" was on display at Trump's Republican convention's Cleveland venue where vendors sold campaign buttons with messages such as "Life's a Bitch—don't vote for one" and "KFC Hillary Special: Two fat thighs, two small breasts . . . left wing." One top-selling t-shirt featured a grinning Donald Trump atop a Harley, as Clinton fell off the bike so one could read the back of Trump's shirt: "IF YOU CAN READ THIS, THE BITCH FELL OFF."

James Comey's innuendo-driven statement in which he announced the "revival" of the investigation into Hillary Clinton's emails, eleven days before election, may have also contributed to her loss (see Wang 2016; Terkel 2016b; Ali 2016.) A second statement from Comey, delivered only two days before the election, cleared her once again but may have come too close to Election Day to have counter-acted any damage to Clinton caused by his earlier announcement (Apuzzo, Schmidt, and Goldman 2016). The impact of Comey's letter is comparatively easy to quantify. At a maximum, it might have shifted the race by three or four percentage points toward Donald Trump, swinging Michigan, Pennsylvania, Wisconsin, and Florida to him, perhaps along with North Carolina and Arizona. At a minimum, its impact might have been only a percentage point or so. Still, because Clinton lost Michigan, Pennsylvania, and Wisconsin by less than one point, the letter was probably enough to change the outcome of the Electoral College (Silver 2017).

Another factor which may have influenced the outcome of the race was Russia's Trump-enabling cyber assaults during the presidential election (see Shane 2017; Krugman 2016e; Blake 2016; Kelley 2016; Lipton, Sanger, and Shane 2016). The Russian hacking and leaking of material, including Hillary Clinton's emails, reverberated "through the presidential election campaign and into the Trump presidency" (Shane 2017). The digital interference was likely a paradigm of strategic character assassination in that it created a "fire hose of stories, true, false and in between, that battered Clinton" on Russian outlets like RT and Sputnik. To illustrate, Facebook officials revealed the shutting down of several hundred accounts they believed were created by a Russian company linked to the

Kremlin and used to buy $100,000 in ads pushing divisive issues during and after the American election campaign.

On Twitter, as on Facebook, Russian "fingerprints" were revealed in "hundreds or thousands" of fake accounts and advertisements that regularly posted what were primarily anti-Clinton messages directed at the candidate personally. A number of the ads questioned the Democratic front-runner's authenticity and referenced "some of the liberal criticisms of her candidacy" as evidence that not only Republicans were divided against her. Others were indirect attempts to weaken her candidacy, including condemnation of Muslim women who supported Clinton and praise for Jill Stein. Still others backed Bernie Sanders and his platform "even after his presidential campaign had ended" while some praised Jill Stein for her "pro-Russian" stance. Many other messages were generated by automated Twitter accounts. While such cyberattacks against Clinton may not have influenced a large enough segment of actual voters to "swing" the election to Trump during the "pre-election melee," Russian voices likely contributed to the success of both Sanders's and Trump's partisan and divisive appeals to their orphaned bases by helping to "fuel a fire of anger and suspicion in a polarized country" (Shane 2017; see also Dawsey 2017; Graham 2017; Sanger and Shane 2016, and Entous, Nakashima, and Miller 2016).

It can also be argued that Clinton's loss to Trump may be configured as punishment for politicians' ignoring the "wants" of their voters, a sort of "payback" to the Republicans (and perhaps as a similar sort of punishment imposed by those Democrats who supported Bernie Sanders) for ignoring a portion of their base so egregiously and for so long:

> If you look past what he's saying, you can see he has become the banner of everyone who is sick of political correctness, sick of being called "racist" for expressing non-liberal opinions, and, most especially, sick of politicians who say whatever they need to to get elected, and then proceed to do whatever the people who paid for their campaign want. It doesn't matter if Trump can't keep his promises. He is punishment for a party that has disenfranchised its political bases so much that they feel their only hope for having their interests represented is— the demagogue (*Time to Fire Trump* 2016).

Another contributing factor to Clinton's loss may be that for years Republican centrists have been tapping into the resentments of struggling middle- and working-class Americans and directing them against the elites that seemed to be in charge, including the media. These included "coddled minorities" and government bureaucrats as well as the judiciary in general and attorneys in particular who benefitted from the redistribution of hard-earned tax dollars. In this view, Trump simply took the anger he generated in his base of disenfranchised voters and transformed those resentments into massive weapons which he relentlessly and successfully used against his enemies, including the GOP establishment (Goldberg 2015).

THE PUBLIC

There is also some indication that the final vote on November 8 was influenced by the nature of the electorate in general: many Americans may not have shared the democratic values embraced by the more conventional political discourse of Hillary Clinton (see Grunwald 2016 and Klein 2016). Some voters may have prioritized concerns other than democratic values as they made their choices for president. For example, members of both Sanders's and Trump's constituencies might have been "simply more attracted" to their candidates who openly and passionately seemed to favor their own constituents' particular religion, race, gender, or wishes rather than a candidate who only represented some abstract "values of democracy" (Stanley 2015). Furthermore, in the current pessimistic political environments of America and Europe, politicians often get punished for appeals to abstract principles or "truth-telling" (Mahbubani 2016). This may be due in part because the ability of some members of the public to comprehend more complex issues or ideological discussion by candidates may be compromised by variations in media literacy and abilities to read or critique such discourse (see Brennan 2016; J. Patterson, 2016; Kerr 2016, and Kirsch et al. 2002).

Voters who lack adequate knowledge, or motive to acquire such, may be manipulated to the degree that some might even "demand policies that contravene their own interests" (Somin 2004). Interestingly, Donald Trump's use of grammar throughout most of his campaign was at the level of a fifth grader. While Allison Smith (2016) suggests less sophisticated language use is not necessarily unusual for politicians, Trump's may stand out:

> He is at times nearly incomprehensible. It can be impossible to sift through his sentence fragments and run-on sentences to find the ideas they contain. In many cases, they don't communicate ideas; they communicate feelings, and often ugly ones.

Moyer (2016) suggests "Trump, for one, seems to intuit that many of his supporters are not grammarians": "I know words; I have the best words . . . but there is no better word than 'stupid'" (Donald Trump speaking during a December 2015 rally, quoted in A. Smith 2016; see also Woffard 2015). Unintentional or not, speaking like an 11-year-old could possibly be another strategy of identification with at least a portion of Trump's targeted constituency. A study conducted by the U.S. Department of Education and the National Institute of Literacy reported that 32 million adults in the United States can't read. That's 14 percent of the population. Twenty-one percent of adults in the United States read below a 5th grade level, and 19 percent of high school graduates can't read (*Illiteracy Statistics* 2016; see also *The US Illiteracy Rate* 2014). It is possible that appeals to democratic values would not resonate—and so would not be generally compelling reasons to vote for a candidate who made such appeals—for those members of the electorate who rejected or were not interested in them, or who could not fully understand them.

Donald Trump's disenfranchised base, because of his ability to "touch their frustration" and inflame their "anger at the establishment, their own party, and America itself," just "did not really care" about blatant inconsistencies in Trump's arguments. C. Edwards III, a distinguished professor of political science at Texas A&M, asserts that that the "low balling" character and "low expectations" of the Republican Party essentially guaranteed the rise of Donald Trump and the defeat of candidates such as Jeb Bush who campaigned on a platform that governing to solve national problems was a priority, which may not have been the case for the Republican Party's electorate:

> Governing requires inclusiveness, substance, and nuance. Success with the Republican electorate seem[ed] to require anti-governing stances, simple answers, and a restricted view of coalitions. [This was] bad for Bush because "celebrity 'trumps' experience in 2016 in the moderate lane" (quoted in Jackson 2016).

Schlueter (2016) suggests the current era of American politics preferences leaders who display "authenticity" rather than "prudence" as they enact their civic responsibilities. In so doing, he foregrounds "a politics based on moderation rather than passion," an imperative if a healthy culture within which self-government may occur is to survive into the twenty-first century:

> Many American citizens today are angry, frustrated, and not a little bit frightened—and with good reason. Every day, news . . . is filled with stories of social, economic, and political breakdown, not to mention warfare, violence, oppression, and deprivation. . . . In the current political climate—where the stakes . . . are so high, yet the conditions for choosing well seem so dim—it may help to take a step back from the immediate spectacle that daily feeds our passions, in order to gain a clearer perspective on the challenges we face. America was born in a series of crises, and fortunately . . . we had statesmen equal to them [including] Jefferson . . . Madison . . . Hamilton [and] Adams [all of whom] left a legacy of practical wisdom that we would do well to hear. Political liberty depends on citizens' interior liberty [which is] only possible with prudence and moderation. Prudence is the intellectual virtue ordered to truth in action. It helps human beings deliberate well about what is truly good, and directs the will to these ends like an arrow to its target. Moderation is the moral virtue that prevents passion from blinding prudence [including] more noble passions like an-

ger, which is related to a love of justice. . . . Prudence and moderation are the handmaids of reason; they stand or fall, together. True statesmen seek to harness passion for the sake of truth, whereas demagogues feed the passions for their own self-aggrandizement. The difficulties of statesmanship and dangers of demagoguery are compounded in an emotivist culture like our own, where every evaluative statement begins with "I feel." Increasingly, it is "passionate intensity" rather than reason that dominates our public discourse.

Situated within and constrained by such a political milieu, Schlueter (2016) concludes it is likely that contemporary candidates who favor and/ or are more adept at preferencing strategies of personality politics over issue-talk may have an edge over those not as skilled or who opt for more traditional and less engaging but more substantive presentations of their candidacies (see Morton 2016 and Nevius 2016; see also Egan 2016). This could also be another possible explanation for Trump's success, Sanders's longevity, and Clinton's loss.

THE OTHER REPUBLICANS

During the primaries, there was also a tendency for the Republican frontrunners such as Marco Rubio and Ted Cruz to avoid criticizing Donald Trump in the hope of winning over his voters later. This was an issue for some concerned—and, as it turned out, visionary—party pundits at the time, particularly as Trump's victories began to multiply:

> Republicans need to take Mr. Trump on. . . . A big majority are decent, compassionate, tolerant people who abhor political violence, bigotry and lying. [They] will be heart-broken if asked to choose in November between a snarling nativist and a Democrat. If the field remains split as it is now, it is possible for Mr. Trump to win with just a plurality of votes. To prevent that, others must drop out. Although we are yet to be convinced by Mr. Rubio, he stands a better chance of beating Mr. Trump than anyone else. All the other candidates . . . should get out of his way. If they decline to do so, it could soon be too late to prevent the party of Abraham Lincoln from being led into a presidential election by Donald Trump (*Time to Fire Trump* 2016)

Leibovich (2016) contends that "the establishment makes for a potent straw man in the hands of people" who may not know "what" they are fighting, only that "they're angry and frustrated." A media working to give at least lip service to "substantive coverage" of a campaign while also exploding a "'good guys' versus 'bad guys' story" for bigger ratings may have been complicit in the success of Trump's and Sanders's outsider strategy in that it privileged political drama over democratic dialogue:

> The media establishment loves "angry and frustrated" as a safe couplet of graveyard words to stand in for more precise and judgmental no-

tions—like maybe "nativist" or "gullible" A strong majority of Trump supporters in South Carolina, for instance, believe that Obama is a Muslim. Yet the media establishment is always careful to lump everyone together as the "angry and frustrated" electorate. To be more specific would jeopardize the solemn commitment to fairness that the media establishment must always strive for.

TRADITIONAL PARTISAN PARTY INFLUENCES

Democrats and Republicans simultaneously and over an extended period of time, if not consciously, may have created the "orphaned" portions of their respective parties to which Bernie Sanders and Donald Trump so effectively appealed in the 2016 presidential race. Goldberg (2015) maintains they did so by ignoring several factors. Franklin Roosevelt offered a modified version of European social-democracy, which is essentially what Sanders meant when he called himself a socialist. The New Deal provided some guarantees of economic security for struggling Americans through social insurance, jobs programs, and major public works. It protected unions, enabling them to achieve a measure of redistribution and economic equality by bargaining for it and relied on regulation to counter excesses of banks and big corporations. In addition, it offered a promise of gradual progress for the disadvantaged through new laws and agencies as well as coalitions drawn from mainstream political and business organizations. This New Deal did not survive the 1960s and 1970s, as social movements, primarily civil rights, divided the United States, resulting in resistance on one side and anger on the other. In addition, demands for women's and LGBT rights produced an increasingly divisive anger-driven "war of cultural values" which splintered the American majority.

The disintegration of American political parties and resulting chaos in leadership, as reflected by the fact that the Republicans had at least 17 candidates, also likely contributed to the outcome of the election. Party dominance began to diminish under pressures from radio and television, which created new ways for candidates to reach others and to do so outside traditional party protocols. The "final blow" was delivered by the Democratic Party's post-1968 election adoption of rules which forced state parties to hold presidential primaries or caucuses. In so doing, party leader influence was reduced; campaign skills became favored over governing skills and inexperienced candidates benefitted. The final result is that the country has "moved from party-based politics to personality-based politics":

> Image and ideology count more than ever because candidates—at all levels of government—try to differentiate themselves from their rivals, both inside and outside their party. Our politicians are increasingly

freelancers, dependent on their own hard work, political savvy, fund-raising ability and public-relations skills (Samuelson 2016).

Peters (2017) argues that, as a political neophyte and former Democrat who was resisted throughout the primaries by the Republican establishment, Donald Trump "put to rest the conventional notion that presidential nominees need the blessing of their party's power brokers to win." Presidential historian Michael Beschloss indicated conditions were "so ripe for such a split" that he was "startled that this had not happened" before. He also suggested Trump's victory proved that "entry is very easy" and that basically all a candidate needed was "money, TV, communication and an issue" (quoted in Peters 2017). According to Geiger (2016), although there are "striking differences" in governing philosophies, Republican and Democratic voters now converge in how they select elected officials. Both constituencies have rejected their respective party establishments as well as the "overall political establishment" through what "appears to be an uncoordinated effort to purge government":

> They are revolting against the entire political industry and seeking elected officials who will not succumb to Washington influences. The American people do not necessarily want bigger or smaller government; they want to overthrow the entire political class (Geiger 2016).

Sanders's and Trump's candidacies could be configured as opposite ends of an American political spectrum. Seagrave (2016) suggests they could be seen as "twin harbingers of a possible American apocalypse," evidence of the "beginning of the end" for American political traditions and "way of life." To illustrate, both focused their campaigns on economic issues; both made no attempt to deny they believed money was the base of "all things good and evil" and both drew their support from a public which considered economic issues to be the most important issue in their own lives as well as facing the United States. The "orphaned electorates" of Bernie Sanders and Donald Trump emerged from the public "left behind" by this Democratic and Republican party breakdown. Each candidate became "the" hero to their partisan base by promising to purge government of entrenched and malignant political leaders and essentially anyone who angered or frightened their partisan followers. Trump supporters may have represented a previously suppressed centric "secular populist group" more interested in celebrity than experience and anti-governing stances than solving national problems (Jackson 2016). However, it is likely that Trump's base developed from the "zombified remnants" of Republican party that was

> really a fraying coalition of three different parties: one that is predominantly socially conservative, one that is intrinsically fiscally threatened, and one that is academically neo-conservative (Kelley 2016).

Sanders's supporters' response to their candidate may have also been triggered by similar divisions which resulted in "democratic disaffection":

> It doesn't take too much effort to see the sub-parties in the Democratic coalition either: there is a blue-collar union party, a party concerned primarily with social liberty, an environmentalist wing, and then perhaps an older more establishment core (Flinders 2016).

The emergence of vigorous "insurgencies" in both parties raised the hope for some that these elements in the Democratic and Republican parties could be joined to create a genuine "cross-party populist movement." In Edsall's (2016) view, the uniting of Trump's and Sanders's orphaned and disenfranchised politics under a common banner had strong appeal, "especially to Democrats on the left":

> Cobble together Trump's older, less educated, lower income, white soft-Republicans, Independents, and his less hard-line conservative voters with Senator Sanders's younger, white, less than $100K family income, Dems and Independents—along with historic Democratic base constituencies and you've got a potent formula for success.

It is likely that the "establishment" factions of both parties "will have a very hard time accommodating the blue-collar native-born Americans" who were the core of Trump's base and a "vital part" of Sanders's (Edsall 2016). Jill Lepore, a professor of American history at Harvard, contends that people who showed up at Sanders and Trump rallies were "wed across the aisle, in bonds of populist unrest." To that end, they joined in revolution against party elites and traditional candidates "anointed" by Democratic and Republican leadership. The unrest has occurred, in part, because of the information technology revolution of the past seven decades, currently being led by the Internet, which has contributed to party disequilibrium. This, in turn, results in an "atomizing of the electorate" at which point "political communication speeds past the last stop where democratic deliberation, the genuine consent of the governed, is possible" (Lepore 2016).

SIGNIFICANCE FOR DEMOCRACIES

As in other eras which have experienced signature mass media innovations, the rapid development of digital information technologies in politics during the 1990s was inspired, in part, by a "utopian sense" that ICTs would also inspire and expand more committed democratic participation (Selnow 1998; see also Graber 1994, Oswald 2009, and West and Dunaway 2017). In particular, some speculated that the 1992 Clinton campaign's decision to actively engage in the "policies and practices of rhetoric in the newly emerging electronic sphere" by distributing transcripts and other campaign materials to USENET and other Listserv groups might reshape the "rhetorical tools and contexts" of presidential leadership.

Such alterations might invigorate democracy by modifying the "conditions of vertical and horizontal political participation by citizens" and so provide instant access to vital rhetorical texts and government documents. Such a "rhetorical presidency," driven by themes of leadership, participation, and access, might recover the "arts of historical memory that are essential to the practice of democracy." Then again, it might not:

> At the very least, in the coming years it will be interesting to observe the oscillation of forces that govern American rhetoric and politics in the information spaces of the future and that will inevitably extend the contestation between a return to localism and the obliteration of boundaries, between community and isolation, between self-government and computerized hegemony, between the electronic commonwealth (Benson 1997, 74; see also Blick 2017).

It has been argued that an informed electorate is a prerequisite for democracy in that if voters do not know what is going on in politics, they cannot rationally exercise control over government policy. In this view, inadequate voter knowledge has two major negative implications for democracy. First, it prevents democratic government from reflecting the will of the people in any meaningful sense, undercutting the "intrinsicist" defense of democracy as a government that reflects the voluntary decisions of the populace. Second,

> voter ignorance imperils the instrumental case for democracy as a regime that serves the interests of the majority, since ignorance potentially opens the door for both elite manipulation of the public and gross policy errors caused by politicians' need to appeal to an ignorant electorate in order to win office (Somin 2004).

Nonetheless, a "relatively stable" level of "extreme ignorance" has persisted even in the face of massive increases in educational attainment to the extent that

> widespread ignorance is not a new phenomenon. . . . But it is striking that knowledge levels have risen very little, if at all, despite rising educational attainment and the increased availability of information through the internet, cable news, and other modern technologies (Somin, 2013).

In this view, political ignorance is a rational act for most of the public, including "most smart people" because they generally have no faith in the system in the first place:

> If your only reason to follow politics is to be a better voter, that turns out not be much of a reason at all. That is because there is very little chance that your vote will actually make a difference to the outcome of

an election (about 1 in 60 million in a presidential race, for example). For most of us, it is rational to devote very little time to learning about politics, and instead focus on other activities that are more interesting or more likely to be useful" (Somin 2013).

The 2016 twin presidential campaigns of Sanders and Trump, grounded as they were by a digitally mediated rhetoric of divisive partisanship, suggest an undemocratic rather than a unifying trajectory for twenty-first-century American democracy that seems to provide no compelling reason for an electorate to "restore" their political faith in the American democracy. Kelley (2016) contends that in almost any other country, there would be "6-8 large, fully functioning parties that would need to coalition build to achieve a majority in the legislature." But in the United States, as evidenced by Sanders's and Trump's impressive (albeit differently successful) campaigns "we have two powerful but widely inaccurate parties that encompass individuals of such varying opinions, they aren't really political parties at all." On the contrary, both were successful because each identified "a select portion of the American populace"—those who "moonlight" as Republicans in Trump's case and Democrats in Sanders's—with laser-targeted, unique, and populist rhetorical appeals of partisanship and division.

Such discursive strategies, however, should be used with caution in future presidential elections. Azari (2014) suggests that recent mandate-driven campaigns have shifted the way that presidents "imagine their constituencies and obligation that indicates an altered logic of governance." Such changes in context and perspective "engage directly with the meaning of representative democracy" in that "the presidency was not designed to represent narrow partisan or ideological concerns" (172). When the political system privileges a president's partisan-centric over public-centered rhetoric, the role of the historical and vital mandate of the president as a trustee of American democracy may be seriously compromised. This is dangerous for American democracy, suggesting that the nation's very electoral process is untrustworthy, its results invalid or not credible. Furthermore, the political system may be additionally compromised when Americans participate so exclusively in a populist vision of a presidency which appeals primarily to "citizen audiences that are likely to be supportive" regardless (Azari 2014).

Flinders (2016) argues that very large numbers of the young people, in particular, in liberal democracies have "so thoroughly" merged "the online with the offline" that most of the entire "human experience" for them is "reflected in, and partially lived through, online networks." It is also significant that social media provides "extraordinarily easy" channels for joining crusades, expressing solidarity and, perhaps most telling, venting outrage. The millennials, as "social-media natives," may be different from previous generations with regard to how they share moral judgments and support each other in "moral campaigns and conflicts." To illustrate, such intentionally targeted members of the electorate may be ignorant of "a basic fact" of democratic political life that "sometimes the 'outsiders' are manifestly worse than the 'insiders'" (Seabrook 2007).

A PERFECT STORM

It can reasonably be argued that a "perfect storm" of coalesced elements, beyond those related to Trump's character assassination rhetoric, had so overwhelmed Clinton by November 8 that it was virtually impossible for her to win. Such elements included Russia's Trump-enabling cyber assaults during the presidential election (see Shane 2017; Krugman 2016e; Blake 2016; Kelley 2016; Lipton, Sanger, and Shane 2016) as well as FBI director James Comey's innuendo-driven rhetorical offenses (see Wang 2016; Terkel 2016b; Ali 2016.). Nonetheless, it is likely that Hillary Clinton's defeat was inevitable in large part because Donald Trump successfully imagined and executed a malignant façade ethos for the Democratic candidate created through digital and socially mediated character assassination.

By dividing the country against itself, Trump and Sanders created a cognitive space within which the marginalized and "orphaned" members of their respective bases simultaneously identified with each in order to unite against Clinton. The divisive rhetoric of Bernie Sanders and Donald Trump appealed to their supporters, who participated in each candidate's narrative versions of a country so in decline that it must engage in a life-or-death fight against itself to be "great again." However, for those who were unsure of this vision or disagree with it, this rhetoric is unsettling.

Conclusion

A Twenty-First-Century Paradigm

Twenty-five centuries of rhetorical theory as well as their own "pugnacious rhetoric" (Sullivan and DeBonis 2017) confirm that Bernie Sanders's and Donald Trump's words matter. In one sense, the rhetorical appeals directed at their respective voter bases fit into the canon of "rhetorical agency," specifically as related to "ownership" of rhetoric and "legitimate performances of rhetoric" (Waite 2012). In this sense "outsider" discourse is situated within a broader category of "otherness" (see Stockdell-Giesler 2010). Both constituencies drew on disillusioned and angry white men to whom Sanders and Trump passionately presented a "rhetoric of otherness." Each created, reinforced, and embellished perceptions of abandonment, anger, and resentment in their respective target audiences. Ultimately, this media-driven rhetorical mechanism so successfully created an "angry orphan" persona for their marginalized electorates that Donald Trump, an outsider with a thirty-year history of extreme wealth, investments, and political party opportunism became America's first "Commander-in-Tweet" (Keith 2016) of the United States.

DEMOCRATIC DISAFFECTION

Both Trump and Sanders shared an anti-establishment ethos which enabled each to embrace a wave of populist support rooted in voters' anger at the political status quo. As one pundit put it, both candidates are attracting "the orphaned vote" consisting of people who don't feel represented by the political ruling class. Donald Trump's surge in the polls initially "baffled" observers, with many suggesting his popularity was merely symptomatic of a reality television-obsessed culture. A candidate's prior political experience once was viewed as a resume builder when running for president, but it is no longer considered to be much of an asset. "Mainstream" candidates such as Jeb Bush and Hillary Clinton struggled to remain relevant and popular in this newest incarnation of an American political environment within which Americans were disgusted with "Washington insider politics." A 2015 poll noted only two percent of voters said they trust government "almost all the time" (Madden). In the seventies, it was voters' lack of trust in the federal government coupled with Jimmy Carter's status as a Washington outsider that led to his surprise nomination and election. A similar dynamic shaped the 2016 election. Clinton, a former Secretary of State and First Lady, and Bush, a son and brother to two former presidents, were stopped, in part, by Sanders's and Trump's discourse, which intensified the animosity of Americans frustrated with the direction of Washington, D.C., and with little faith in a traditional nominating system against which both outsider candidates incessantly railed. Madden (2015) argues such public indignation is understandable if voters believe a system is corrupt and rigged against them to benefit elites, regardless of party affiliation. Ultimately, the discursive vision created by Sanders and Trump, of an America over which Hillary Clinton ruled as a dominating, immoral, and insider female politician, opened the door for the ultimate outsider candidate, Donald Trump, to dominate the playing field and win the presidency (Madden 2015).

Rhetorical Substance

While the major premise of this text is that Trump and Sanders were substantially united in how they campaigned against Hillary Clinton to their respective segments of the American electorate, it is important to note that the partisanship evidenced in Campaign 2016 was about issues in substance rather than style. What their campaigns shared is critical to an understanding of how they unfolded as well as the effect of these campaigns on American democracy in that both embody what could be an historic showdown between the respective parties and their supporters. Trump spoke for a segment of the Republican base "that's broken free of the traditional Republican message" while Sanders represented a traditional Democratic message, but one that "has long since been abandoned by the party's base" (Goldberg 2015).

As such, care should be taken to unpack and counter what Krugman (2016a) identifies as a "false equivalency" argument that this substantive divide was no different between "Trump Republicans" and "Sanders Democrats" who were essentially the same people:

> I still encounter people on the left (although never on the right) who claim that there's no big difference between Republicans and Democrats, or at any rate "establishment" Democrats. . . . When we talk about partisanship, then, we're not talking about arbitrary teams, we're talking about a deep divide on values and policy. How can anyone not be "partisan" in the sense of preferring one of these visions? And it's up to you to decide which version you prefer. Beyond that, there are huge differences in tactics and attitudes. . . . So how does this get resolved? One answer could be a Republican sweep. . . . Or maybe you believe—based on no evidence I'm aware of—that a populist rising

from the left is ready to happen any day now (Krugman 2016a; see also Borosage 2015).

It is important, therefore, to remember that although both men waged campaigns that were aesthetically and affectively similar, if not mirrored images of the other, what they asked of their particular bases was substantively different.

Others are concerned that, taken together, the "outsider" campaigns of Bernie Sanders and Donald Trump have unsettled the foundations of both the Democratic and Republican parties. The emergence and popularity of anti-establishment and divisive figures such as former Democrat Trump on the right and former Independent Sanders on the left has revealed the desire on the part of millions of Americans for disruption in both parties. Michael Steele, a former chairman of the Republican National Committee, maintains that as a president who has "essentially borrowed the Republican label," Donald Trump "plays with whomever he wants," an independence which not only is "unsettling the very foundation of the party," but has "already started to reshape the landscape" (quoted in Peters 2017).

Furthermore, that Donald Trump won the 2016 American presidential campaign is significant not only with regard to the party system but to American democracy as it has been configured for over two centuries. Allen (2016) believes that Trump's decisions about how to run his campaign as well as "run the country" once he became president are indications that he "has no respect for the basic rights that are the foundation of constitutional democracy, nor for the requirements of decency necessary to sustain democratic citizenship." This is compounded by the reality that such a democracy cannot survive without an expectation that the people require reasonable arguments that "bring the truth to light," which was not a priority in his campaign, nor does it appear to be as he enacts his presidency.

PRIVILEGING DIVISIVENESS

This text suggests that the 2016 presidential campaign was strategically orchestrated to privilege divisiveness over consensus as a quick fix for a big win but little concern for the formidable threat such a campaign posed to American's shared liberties. James Madison, writing in 1787, warned against the "violence of faction" in the then new confederation of American states and eloquently argued that constituting the nation as a representative democracy would fortify the United States against such a threat:

> Among the numerous advantages promised by a well-constructed Union, none deserves to be more accurately developed than its tendency

> to break and control the violence of faction. . . . A republic, by which I
> mean a government in which the scheme of representation takes
> place . . . promises the cure for which we are seeking. . . . The effect [is]
> to refine and enlarge the public views by passing them through the
> medium of citizens, whose wisdom may best discern the true interest
> of their country [and] whose enlightened views and virtuous senti-
> ments render them superior to local prejudices and to schemes of injus-
> tice (Hamilton, Madison and Jay 1787, 41–47).

In Stanley's view (2015), the principles of American government, as articulated by Madison, Alexander Hamilton, and John Jay, three of the Constitution's framers and ratifiers, mandated leaders be elected who "best
represented the values of democracy." To that end, "an election campaign is supposed to present candidates seeking to show that they have
the common interests of all citizens at heart."

A Twitter Presidency

Donald Trump has become the United States' first "Twitter president"
because his digital campaign team successfully marketed into the presidency a candidate "the majority of Americans did not want" but also
whose primary means of communication was a social networking service
where users interact through messages limited to 140 characters (Halpern
2017). Trump's ascension was given a boost by a "multiple political personality disorder" which manifested as "rhetorical schizophrenia" (Gerson 2017) of discursive expediency enacted primarily through digital social media. While not itself an entirely unique campaign strategy, that
Trump's reliance on this technique when coupled with what many have
asserted is a post-election "abnormal handling of the presidency" is dis-
turbing (see Cohen, Roger 2017; Bui et al. 2017; J. Goldberg 2017; and
Trump's Tweets 2017). Future presidential campaigns will build on the
lessons from this presidency, which include that it actually pays to only
please some of the people some of the time, and the rest simply don't
count.

In an August 2017 interview, Secretary of State Rex Tillerson not only
called into question the credibility of Trump's statements but also whether the president spoke for himself rather than American values. In the
televised interview, Fox News host Chris Wallace reported that a United
Nations committee had criticized Trump's apparent defense of white su-
premacists at a rally in Charlottesville, Virginia, earlier in the month.
Though he denied Trump's words made it difficult to defend American
diplomacy abroad, the Secretary of State refused to deny that he was
attempting to distance himself and the State Department from the president's comments:

> I don't believe anyone doubts the American people's values, or the
> commitment of the American government, or the government's agen-

cies to advancing those values and defending those values [but with regard to the president's values] the president speaks for himself" (Tillerson quoted in Tani 2017).

When Wallace asked if Tillerson was distancing himself from Trump's comments on Charlottesville, Tillerson referenced the position he had made clear in an earlier State Department speech:

> We all know hate is not an American value. Nowhere is it an American value. We do honor, protect, and defend freedom of speech, First Amendment rights. It's what sets us apart from every other government regime in the world, in allowing people a right to expression. These are good things. But we do not honor, nor do we promote or accept hate speech in any form. And those who embrace it poison our public discourse and they damage the very country that they claim to love. So we condemn racism, bigotry in all its forms. Racism is evil; it is antithetical to America's values. It's antithetical to the American idea (Tillerson 2017).

DIGITAL INTERVENTION

There are suggestions for industry-centric interventions to distinguish between authentic and manufactured news and other cyber-syndromes. For example, network gateways to determine message origins could be developed, much as one "authenticates" those one hears but cannot see by sound of voice, vocabulary, and interests (O'Malley and Levin 2017). Self-protecting behaviors may also shield individual Americans from digital character assassination such as that enacted by Donald Trump's cyber-assault against Hillary Clinton. These include nurturing for the "internet savvy"—learning "preventative" skills for strategic reputation management and, for those less "savvy," skills for managing digital platforms such as Twitter and Facebook. Specific strategies include keeping up with changes in cyberspace by reading online sources to become more informed about social media. Another strategy requires an introspective assessment of personal vulnerabilities which might be exploited by a potential digital assassinator. It may also be wise to assess one's "actual self" in terms of one's "profile or personal brand" as constituted online, after which a "reputational cushion" could be designed "to absorb blows" against a public persona.

"Regulating the ether" (a term for radio "in its early days" representing one-to-many communication) is also a possibility in that the Internet "acts in essence like radio" but with "a nearly infinite number of broadcast channels" by finding one or two themes "to promote about yourself" and "stick to them." Finally, in order to "level the playing field," while appeals to justice or fairness will likely fail to win vindication, one may "call on friends, both real and virtual" to help:

Being actively connected to a community of friends is the greatest resource in the face of a digital assassin. They can [alert] when you are
making a digital mistake [and] defend when you . . . come under attack, with a credible counter (Torrenzano and Davis 2011, 210–230).

DIALOGIC INTERVENTION

Twenty-four centuries ago, Plato warned that the alchemy responsible
for producing a democracy could also produce tyranny, observing that
an "insatiable thirst" for the elements contained in democracy could also
destroy it (1871, 2005). A disconcerting legacy emerges from this study of
the divisive partisanship rhetoric of Bernie Sanders and Donald Trump:
the American presidency may be won by communication that counters
rather than epitomizes the best values of American democracy. Barrett
(1991) spoke of a "condition" identified as a "rhetorical maladaptation," a
type of discursive narcissism, an excessive, self-serving behavior which
causes ineffectiveness and incivility in social interaction of any sort, including "on the public platform" (ix). Such rhetors typically reveal behaviors against or from others—or "with others in disastrous fusion."
Furthermore "uncivil people" catch others in the "web of misery" which
is both constituted by and a contributing factor to "rhetorical maladaptation" so that:

> [They are] never unaccompanied. Whether acting from regression or
> inadequate growth, they always find others to be with—others who
> come to them. Together they display qualities of incivility (151).

Since a "healthy" rhetorical process is a function of civility (146–7) it
follows that "the facilitation of civility is a rhetorical function" (149). It
may be that the rhetorical choices of Sanders and Trump, which preferenced division and partisanship over consensus and cooperation, were
reasonable (if not uncivil and possibly anti-democratic) responses to an
American public and political environment already rhetorically mala-
dapted long before either considered becoming an American president:

> Indeed, the audience shares the problem, for narcissism as a rhetorical
> pathology is sender-receiver pathology. When in support of unsocial
> behavior of others, audiences seek satisfaction of their own narcissistic
> needs (154).

It has been argued that Bernie Sanders and Donald Trump were both
intentionally and dangerously disruptive, powerful candidates who
"welcomed chaos for its own sake." In this view, "excessive power,"
whether "in an executive or in a mob" has historically been counterbal-
anced by a constitutional democracy, the "ultimate guardians" of which
are American voters. The 2016 presidential campaign suggests the electorate may be ignoring their custodial responsibilities to democracy by

turning to demagogues in both parties. Flinders (2016) believes a re-connecting of the American "democratic or political imagination" must occur in order to compensate for the descent of representative democracy into "representation-via-political tribe." Kruger and Dunning report that improving the critical thinking skills of people who are "completely unaware that they are unaware" increases their "metacognitive competence" and enables them to recognize the limitations of their abilities caused by the original cognitive bias of illusory superiority (Kruger and Dunning 1999, 1121). Consequently, a systematic, incremental, and even initially anecdotal reinstatement or, in some cases, introduction of critical thinking skills into public awareness may illuminate the illusion, apparently shared by many Americans on both sides of the political aisle, that their democracy is best served by embracing divisive and partisan populism rather than mindful and consensus-driven dialogue.

THE GOOD AUDIENCE

Certainly, narratives produced by "the right leadership" may counter and even deflect the populism that in some national cultures, including that of the United States, threatens to slow down, if not stop entirely, the momentum of democracy (Mahbubani 2016). Conversely, the development of "the good audience" may be the better option as a rhetorical solution to what may primarily be a rhetorical problem. Burke (1969, 1984) previewed this notion when he suggested identification of a rhetor and an audience as both process and end, and a necessary and critical response to the reality that humans are distinct and divided from one another but must nonetheless "come together." This "consubstantiality" or sharing of "common attributes, values, needs, and feelings" is the prerequisite necessary for individuals to experience and enact the human community. "Knowledgeable and aware, self-respecting, courageous, able, independent, responsible, free, and willing to engage, the good audience assumes its role civilly" (Barrett 1991, 156).

Some of the attributes of such an audience include that it has a "clearly realized purpose" (as in "to enable democracy"); that it makes itself "available for interaction" (as in exposing itself to ideas or arguments); that it possesses "self-respect" (as in appreciating independence and objectivity). Also, the "good audience" engages in "social awareness" (as in realizing others' needs); is "responsible for its own behavior" (as in owning its judgments); is "vigilant" and recognizes "the existence in this life of powerful, clashing forces" (as in recognizing diversity) (155–156).

Based on this model, perhaps attempts to develop "the American electorate" as a "good audience" may be the rhetorical solution to the "rhetorical maladaptation" evidenced by Sanders's and Trump's choices to wage campaigns driven by partisan divisiveness rather than deliberation and civil decision making:

> [It is] the model of an active, self-respecting, rhetorically disposed person or group who in their rhetorical maturity selectively confirm and disconfirm the behavior of people with whom they relate. The development of good audiences in influential roles of good parents, good teachers, good officials, good therapists, and good citizens everywhere should be one of the nation's highest educational priorities (Barrett 1991, x).

The challenge is to develop (or reinvent) a paradigm for imagining the remaining presidential campaigns of the twenty-first century so that Plato's warning does not become democracy's trajectory in the United States.

There are three take-aways which speak directly to the future of American elections which may be drawn from this study of Bernie Sanders's and Donald Trump's discursive exploitation of their respective segments of America's "orphaned electorate." First, subsequent campaigns and their candidates must be savvy producers and consumers of digitally mediated political rhetoric. Second, political actors—particularly presidential candidates, along with their constituents—must interact within political cultures created by dialogic rather than divisive voices. Finally, and perhaps most importantly, as evidenced in particular by the forty-fifth United States president's rhetorical behavior thus far, the actions of politicians and publics must be informed by a respect for and allegiance to the country's constitutional democracy as enacted through a rhetoric of civility, decency, and justice.

References

Achen, Christopher and Larry Bartels. 2016. "Do Sanders' Supporters Favor His Policies?" *The New York Times,* May 23, 2016. https://www.nytimes.com/2016/05/23/opinion/campaign-stops/do-sanders-supporters-favor-his-policies.html

Alcindor, Yamiche. 2016a. "Bernie Sanders Facing Pressure Over Supporter's Actions in Nevada." *The New York Times,* May 17, 2016. http://www.nytimes.com/2016/05/18/us/politics/bernie-sanders-supporters-nevada.html?action=click&contentCollection=Politics&module=RelatedCoverage&region=EndOfArticle&pgtype=article

———. 2016b. "Bernie Sanders Refuses to Concede Nomination to Hillary Clinton." *The New York Times,* June 12, 2016. http://www.nytimes.com/2016/06/13/us/politics/bernie-sanders-campaign.html

Ali, Safia. 2016. "The 'Comey Effect': Where Does the FBI Director Stand As Election Dust Settles?" *NBC News,* November 19, 2016. http://www.nbcnews.com/news/us-news/comey-effect-where-does-fbi-director-stand-election-dust-settles-n680076

Allen, Danielle. 2016. "The Moment of Truth: We Must Stop Trump." *The Washington Post,* February 21, 2016. https://www.washingtonpost.com/opinions/moment-of-truth-we-must-stop-trump/2016/02/21/0172e788-d8a7–11e5–925f-1d10062cc82d_story.html

Alperstein, Robin. 2016. "On Becoming Anti-Bernie." *Medium.com,* April 17, 2016. http://medium.com/@robinalperstein/on-becoming-anti-bernie-ee87943ae699#.ie23r71cu

Alterman, Eric. 2016. "Distorting the 2016 Election Coverage." *The Nation,* June 2, 2016. https://www.thenation.com/article/how-false-equivalence-is-distorting-the-2016-election-coverage/

"Americanism: A Presidential Gambit." 2016. *The Economist ("Espresso"),* July 18, 2016. https://espresso.economist.com/9e7ba617ad9e69b39bd0c29335b79629

Anderson, Karrin Vasby. 2016. "'Bern the Witch' and 'Trump that Bitch': Likability / Loathability on the Presidential Campaign Trail." *Spectra* 52, no. 3&4 (September / November 2016): 20–26.

"ANES Time Series Study." 2016. *American National Election Studies.* http://www.electionstudies.org/studypages/anes_timeseries_2016/anes_timeseries_2016.htm

Apuzzo, Matt, Michael S. Schmidt, and Adam Goldman. 2016. "Emails Warrant No New Action Against Hillary Clinton, F.B.I. Director Says." *The New York Times,* November 6, 2016. https://www.nytimes.com/2016/11/07/us/politics/hilary-clinton-male-voters-donald-trump.html

Arendt, Hannah. 1968. *Men in Dark Times.* New York: Harcourt Brace and Co.

———. 1963. *Eichmann in Jerusalem: A Report on the Banality of Evil.* New York: Viking Books.

Azari, Julia. 2014. *Delivering the People's Message: The Changing Politics of the Presidential Mandate.* Ithaca: Cornell University Press.

Bakhtin, Mikhail. 1941. *Rabelais and His World.* Bloomington: Indiana University Press.

Ball, Charing. 2016. "Why Bernie Sanders Lost, Part I: He Was Unrealistic About Race." *Madamenoire.com,* June 9, 2016. http://madamenoire.com/701608/bernie-sanders-lost

Barbaro, Michael, and Yamiche Alcindor. 2016 "Hillary Clinton Made History, but Bernie Sanders Stubbornly Ignored It." *The New York Times,* June 8, 2016. http://

www.nytimes.com/2016/06/09/us/politics/bernie-sanders-campaign.html?smprod=nytcore-iphone&smid=nytcore-iphone-share

Barrett, Harold. 1991. *Rhetoric and Civility: Human Development, Narcissism, and the Good Audience.* Albany: State University of New York Press.

Bell, Kamau W., Armando Iannucci, Michelle King, Robert King, and Shonda Rhimes. 2013. "Television and Politics." *The New Yorker,* October 14, 2013. http://www.newyorker.com/culture/new-yorker-festival/television-and-politics

Benjamin, Walter. 1936. "The Work of Art in the Age of Mechanical Reproduction." In *Illuminations,* edited by Hannah Arendt, 217–252. New York: Random House.

Benson, Thomas. 1997. "Desktop Demos: New Communication Technologies and the Future of the Rhetorical Presidency." In *Beyond the Rhetorical Presidency,* edited by Martin Medhurst, 50–74. College Station: Texas A&M University.

Bereznak, Alyssa. 2017. "The Digital Presidency of Donald Trump." *The Ringer,* February 8, 2017. https://www.theringer.com/2017/2/8/16036778/donald-trump-digital-presidency-barack-obama-e3072777675c

"Bernie Sanders' Economic Policy: A Vote for What?" 2016. *The Economist,* February 11, 2016. https://www.economist.com/news/united-states/21692895-health-care-costs-and-high-taxes-would-sink-sanders-economic-plan-vote-what

"Bernie Sanders' Supporters Give Trump the Edge in Florida Poll." 2016. *Sunshine State News,* October 6, 2016. http://www.sunshinestatenews.com/story/bernie-sanders-supporters-give-trump-edge-florida-poll

"Bernie Quotes for a Better World." 2017. *Better World.* http://www.betterworld.net/quotes/bernie/bernie4.htm

Berry, Lorraine. 2016. "Umberto Eco on Donald Trump: 14 Ways of Looking at a Fascist." *LitHub,* February 29, 2016. http://lithub.com/umberto-eco-on-donald-trump-14-ways-of-looking-at-a-fascist/

Billet, Alexander. 2016. "Donald Trump and the Aesthetics of Fascism. *In These Times,* January 28, 2016. Retrieved from http://inthesetimes.com/article/18807/donald-trump-and-the-aesthetics-of-fascism.

Blake, Aaron. 2016b. "The CIA Concluded That Russia Worked to Elect Trump. Republicans Now Face an Impossible Choice." *The Washington Post,* December 9, 2016. https://www.washingtonpost.com/news/the-fix/wp/2016/12/09/the-cia-concluded-russia-worked-to-elect-trump-republicans-now-face-an-impossible-choice/?utm_term=.e3c1270be373

Blick, Andrew. 2017. "The Internet and Democracy: An Historical Perspective." *History and Policy,* May 21, 2017. http://www.historyandpolicy.org/policy-papers/papers/the-internet-and-democracy-an-historical-perspective

Blow, Charles M. 2016a. "Demagogue for President." *The New York Times,* March 3, 2016. http://www.nytimes.com/2016/03/03/opinion/campaign-stops/demagogue-for-president.html

———. 2016b. "'Bernie or Bust' is Bonkers." *The New York Times,* March 21, 2016. http://www.nytimes.com/2016/03/31/opinion/campaign-stops/bernie-or-bust-is-bonkers.html?recp=17&_r=0

———. 2016c. "A Trump-Sanders Coalition? Nah." *The New York Times,* May 2, 2016. https://www.nytimes.com/2016/05/02/opinion/a-trump-sanders-coalition-nah.html

Bohanan, Rebecca. 2016. "The Bernie vs. Hillary Battle All Boils Down to Sexism." *The Huffington Post,* May 25, 2016. http://www.huffingtonpost.com/rebecca-bohanan/the-bernie-vs-hillary-bat_b_10132260.html

Bordo, Susan. 2017. "The Destruction of Hillary Clinton: Sexism, Sanders and the Millennial Feminists." *The Guardian,* April 2, 2017. https://www.theguardian.com/us-news/commentisfree/2017/apr/03/the-destruction-of-hillary-clinton-sexism-sanders-and-the-millennial-feminists

Borosage, Robert. 2015. "Sanders and Trump: The Populist and the Demagogue." *OurFuture.org,* August 20, 2015. https://ourfuture.org/20150820/sanders-and-trump-the-populist-and-the-demagogue

Bouie, Jamelle. 2015. "Donald Trump is a Fascist." *Slate*, November 25, 2015 http://www.slate.com/articles/news_and_politics/politics/2015/11/donald_trump_is_a_fascist_it_is_the_political_label_that_best_describes.html

Brennan, Jason. 2016. "Trump Won Because Voters Were Ignorant, Literally." *Foreign Policy*, November 10, 2016. http://foreignpolicy.com/2016/11/10/the-dance-of-the-dunces-trump-clinton-election-republican-democrat/

Brooks, David. 2016. "The Governing Cancer of Our Time." *The New York Times*, February 26, 2016. https://www.nytimes.com/2016/02/26/opinion/the-governing-cancer-of-our-time.html

Bruni, Frank. 2016. "The Cult of Sore Losers." *The New York Times*, April 27, 2016. http://www.nytimes.com/2016/04/27/opinion/the-cult-of-sore-losers.html

Budowsky, Brent. 2015. "Bernie Sanders, Ron Paul and the Social Media Revolution." *The Hill*, August 19, 2015. http://thehill.com/blogs/pundits-blog/presidential-campaign/251465-bernie-sanders-ron-paul-and-the-social-media

Bui, Quoctrung, Claire Miller, and Kevin Quealy. 2017. "Just How Abnormal is the Trump Presidency? Rating 20 Events." *The New York Times*, February 27, 2017. https://www.nytimes.com/interactive/2017/02/27/upshot/whats-normal-whats-important-a-ranking-of-20-events-in-the-trump-administration.html

Bump, Philip. 2016a. "How the Internet Has Democratized Democracy, to Bernie Sanders's Benefit." *The Washington Post*, February 18, 2016. https://www.washingtonpost.com/news/the-fix/wp/2016/02/18/how-the-internet-has-democratized-democracy-to-bernie-sanderss-benefit/?tid=a_inl&utm_term=.3991b1384f45

———. 2016b. "How Bernie Sanders is Hijacking the Democratic Party to Be Elected as an Independent." *The Washington Post*, March 15, 2016. https://www.washingtonpost.com/news/the-fix/wp/2016/03/15/how-bernie-sanders-is-hijacking-the-democratic-party-to-be-elected-as-an-independent/?utm_term=.c1953fa36cd4

———. 2016c. "White Male Democrats Have Disproportionately Voted Against Hillary Clinton for Eight Years Running." *The Washington Post*, May 5, 2016. https://www.washingtonpost.com/news/the-fix/wp/2016/05/05/white-male-democrats-have-disproportionately-voted-against-hillary-clinton-for-eight-years-running/?utm_term=.19234e99330c

———. 2016d. "Trump Got the Most GOP Votes Ever—Both For and Against Him—and Other Fun Facts." *The Washington Post*, June 8, 2016. https://www.washingtonpost.com/news/the-fix/wp/2016/06/08/donald-trump-got-the-most-votes-in-gop-primary-history-a-historic-number-of-people-voted-against-him-too/

———. 2016e. "Bernie Sanders' Big Convention Speech Was the Same Speech He Gave When He First Endorsed Hillary Clinton." *The Washington Post*, July 25, 2016. https://www.washingtonpost.com/news/the-fix/wp/2016/07/25/bernie-sanderss-big-convention-speech-was-the-same-speech-he-gave-when-he-first-endorsed-hillary-clinton/?tid=a_inl&utm_term=.d29ce9f07ccd

Burke, Kenneth. 1931. *Counter-Statement*. New York: Harcourt, Brace & Company.

———. 1966. *Language as Symbolic Action*. Berkeley: University of California Press.

———. 1969. *A Rhetoric of Motives*. Berkeley: University of California Press.

———. 1984. *Permanence and Change*. 3rd ed. Berkeley: University of California Press.

———. 1990. "From a Rhetoric of Motives. In *The Rhetorical Tradition*, edited by Patricia Bizzell and Bruce Herzberg. Boston: Bedford Books.

Burns, Alexander. 2016. "Anti-Trump Republicans Call for a Third-Party Option." *The New York Times*, March 2, 2016. https://www.nytimes.com/2016/03/03/us/politics/anti-donald-trump-republicans-call-for-a-third-party-option.html

Burns, Nicholas. 2016. "We Need Hillary for President." *USA Today*, February 19, 2016. http://www.usatoday.com/story/opinion/2016/02/18/hillary-clinton-president-foreign-policy-crises-sanders-bush-kasich-nicholas-burns/80472346/

Busch, Andrew. 1997. *Outsiders and Openness in the Presidential Nominations System.* Pittsburgh: University of Pittsburgh Press.

Camosy, Charles. 2016. "Trump Won Because College-Educated Voters Were Out of Touch." *The Washington Post,* November 9, 2016. https://www.washingtonpost.com/posteverything/wp/2016/11/09/trump-won-because-college-educated-americans-are-out-of-touch/?utm_term=.cdfdf5502a6b

"Candidates Differ in Their Use of Social Media." 2016. *Pew Research Center,* July 18, 2016. http://www.journalism.org/2016/07/18/candidates-differ-in-their-use-of-social-media-to-connect-with-the-public/

Capkronus. 2016. "Harvard Study Confirms Anti-Clinton Media Bias." *DailyKos,* June 26, 2016. https://www.dailykos.com/stories/2016/6/26/1542758/-Harvard-Study-Confirms-Anti-Clinton-Media-Bias

Carney, Dan. 2016. "The White Revolt Over Dashed Expectations." *USA Today*, March 31, 2016. https://www.usatoday.com/story/opinion/2016/03/28/whites-blacks-latinos-presidential-election-donald-trump-bernie-sanders-hillary-clinton-column/81985562/

Cassidy, John. 2016. "Bernie Sanders and the New Populism." *The New Yorker*, February 2, 2016. https://www.newyorker.com/news/john-cassidy/bernie-sanders-and-the-new-populism

Chait, Jonathan. 2015. "How 'Negative Partisanship' Has Transformed American Politics." *New York Magazine*, April 17, 2015. http://nymag.com/daily/intelligencer/2015/04/negative-partisanship-has-transformed-politics.html

———. 2016. "The Case Against Bernie Sanders." *New York Magazine*, January 18, 2016. http://nymag.com/daily/intelligencer/2016/01/case-against-bernie-sanders.html

Charen, Mona. 2016. "Day of the Demagogues." *The National Review*, February 10, 2016. http://www.nationalreview.com/article/431122/bernie-sanders-donald-trump-wall-street-immigration-demagoguery

Chaykowski, Kathleen. 2016. "Why Bernie Sanders's Social Media Followers Are More Engaged Than Donald Trump's." *Forbes,* March 15, 2016. https://www.forbes.com/sites/kathleenchaykowski/2016/03/25/why-bernie-sanderss-social-media-followers-are-more-engaged-than-donald-trumps/#c921fc103de2

Childress, Sarah. 2016. "Study: Election Coverage Skewed by 'Journalistic Bias'." *Frontline*, July 12, 2016. http://www.pbs.org/wgbh/frontline/article/study-election-coverage-skewed-by-journalistic-bias/

Chozick, Amy and Ashley Parker. 2016. "Donald Trump's Gender Based Attacks on Hillary Clinton Have Calculated Risks." *The New York Times,* April 28, 2016. https://www.nytimes.com/2016/04/29/us/politics/hillary-clinton-donald-trump-women.html

Ciruli, Floyd. 2016. "2016 is the Year of the Outsider in Presidential Politics." *The Denver Post,* January 29, 2016. http://www.denverpost.com/perspective/ci_29449393/ciruli-2016-is-year-outsider-presidential-politics

Clinton, Hillary. 2016. "Hillary Clinton's DNC Speech: Full Text." *CNN,* July 19, 2016. http://cnn.com/2016/07/28/politics/hillary-clinton-speech-prepared-remarks-transcript/index.html

Clymer, Charles. 2016. "The Pettiness of the Angry White Male." *Medium.com,* May 16, 2016. https://medium.com/@cmclymer/the-pettiness-of-the-angry-white-male-58bcc970021d#.43r0kdvow

Cohen, Richard. 2006. "Digital Lynch Mob." *The Washington Post*, May 9, 2006. http://www.washingtonpost.com/wp-dyn/content/article/2006/05/08/AR2006050801323.html

Cohen, Roger. 2016. "The Trump-Berlusconi Syndrome." *The New York Times*, March 15, 2016. http://www.nytimes.com/2016/03/15/opinion/the-trump-berlusconi-syndrome.html

———. 2017. "The Abnormal Presidency of Donald Trump." *The New York Times,* January 31, 2017. https://www.nytimes.com/2017/01/31/opinion/the-abnormal-presidency-of-donald-trump.html

Cooper, Matthew. 2016a. "Why Bernie Sanders Should Condemn His Worst Supporters." *Newsweek,* May 17, 2016. http://www.newsweek.com/sanders-kentucky-oregon-nevada-clinton-barbara-boxer-death-threats-461008

———. 2016b. "How Donald Trump Courted White Americans to Victory." *Newsweek,* November 9, 2016. http://www.newsweek.com/2016/11/18/donald-trump-white-working-class-voters-election-2016–519095.html

Corasaniti, Nick. 2016. "Bernie Sanders Takes to Social Media to Reach Younger Voters." *The New York Times,* February 9, 2016.

Cottle, Michelle. 2016. "The Era of 'The Bitch' is Coming: A Hillary Clinton Presidential Victory Promises to Usher in a New Age of Public Misogyny." *The Atlantic,* August 17, 2016. http://www.theatlantic.com/politics/archive/2016/08/the-era-of-the-bitch-is-coming/496154/

Cupp, S.E. 2016. "Trump Ducks Sanders Debate and We Lose." *CNN,* May 27, 2016. http://www.cnn.com/2016/05/27/opinions/sanders-trump-debate-cupp/

Daou, Peter. 2016a. "GUT-CHECK: If You Hate Hillary More Than You Love Bernie, Take a Hard Look at Yourself." *Blue Nation Review,* March 31, 2016. http://bluenationreview.com/if-you-hate-hillary-more-than-you-love-bernie/

———. 2016b. "SCORCHED: Bernie's Campaign Manager Throws a Bomb About Hillary and Young Voters." *Blue Nation Review,* April 5, 2016. http://bluenationreview.com/bernies-campaign-manager-throws-a-bomb-about-hillary-and-young-voters/

Davis, Lanny. 2016. "Media Bias on Polls Against Clinton Now Indisputable." *The Des Moines Register,* January 20, 2016. http://www.desmoinesregister.com/story/opinion/columnists/caucus/2016/01/20/media-bias-polls-against-clinton-now-indisputable/79076226/

Dawsey, Josh. 2017. "Russian-Funded Facebook Ads Backed Stein, Sanders, and Trump." *Politico,* September 26, 2017. http://www.politico.com/story/2017/09/26/facebook-russia-trump-sanders-stein-243172?wpmm=1&wpisrc=nl_daily202

DeCosta-Klipa, Nik. 2016. "This Harvard Study Both Confirms and Refutes Bernie Sanders's Complaints About the Media." *Boston.com,* May 10, 2016. https://www.boston.com/news/politics/2016/06/14/harvard-study-confirms-refutes-bernie-sanderss-complaints-media

Desilver, Drew. 2016. "Turnout Was High in the 2016 Primary Season, But Just Short of a 2008 Record." *Pew Research Center,* June 10, 2015. http://www.pewresearch.org/fact-tank/2016/06/10/turnout-was-high-in-the-2016-primary-season-but-just-short-of-2008-record/

"Despite What Candidates Say, It's Not 'Mourning in America.'" 2016. *USA Today,* February 29, 2016. 7A.

Diamond, Jeremy. 2017. "Trump Retweets GIF of Him Hitting Clinton With Golf Ball." *CNN,* September 17, 2017. http://www.cnn.com/2017/09/17/politics/trump-tweet-clinton/index.html

Dickinson, Matthew. 2015. "Trump Isn't Sanders Isn't Trump." *U.S. News and World Report,* September 2, 2015. http://www.usnews.com/opinion/blogs/opinion-blog/2015/09/02/donald-trump-and-bernie-sanders-are-not-similar-2016-candidates

"Digital News Developments in U.S. Presidential Campaigns, 2000–2016." 2017. *Pew Research Center,* July 18, 2017. http://www.journalism.org/2016/07/18/digital-news-developments-in-u-s-presidential-campaigns-2000–2016/

"Donald Trump Reprises Campaign Attacks, Declares Hillary Clinton 'Guilty as Hell.'" 2017. *The Huffington Post,* January 13, 2017. http://www.huffingtonpost.com/entry/trump-reprises-clinton-campaign-attack_us_5878e365e4b09281d0ea6629

Dovere, Edward-Isaac. 2016. "Trump's New Aim: Poison a Clinton Presidency." *Politico,* August 29, 2016. http://www.politico.com/story/2016/08/trump-clinton-poison-conspiracy-227485

————. 2017. "Trump's Divisive Unity Plea." *Politico,* May 18, 2017. http://www.politico.com/story/2017/05/18/trump-unity-plea-238582

Dovere, Edward-Isaac and Gabriel Debenedetti. 2016. "Inside the Bitter Last Days of Bernie's Revolution." *Politico,* June 7, 2016. http://www.politico.com/story/2016/06/bernie-sanders-campaign-last-days-224041

Dunning, David. 2016. "The Psychological Quirk That Explains Why You Love Donald Trump." *Politico,* May 25, 2016. http://www.politico.com/magazine/story/2016/05/donald-trump-supporters-dunning-kruger-effect-213904

Dutton, Sarah, Jennifer DePinto, Fred Backus, Kabir Khanna, and Anthony Salvanto. 2017. "Russian Interference in the 2016 Election." *CBS News,* January 18, 2017. https://www.cbsnews.com/news/most-americans-think-russia-tried-to-interfere-in-presidential-election/

Eco, Umberto. 1995. "Ur-Fascism." *The New York Review of Books,* June 22, 1995. http://www.nybooks.com/articles/1856

Edelman, Murray. 1988. *Constructing the Political Spectacle.* London: The University of Chicago Press.

Editorial Board. 2016. "Editorial: How Donald Trump Tends His Media Blacklist." *The New York Times,* June 16, 2016. http://www.nytimes.com/2016/06/16/opinion/how-donald-trump-tends-his-media-blacklist.html?smprod=nytcore-iphone&smid=nytcore-iphone-share

Edsall, Thomas B. 2016. "The Trump-Sanders Fantasy" *The New York Times,* February 24, 2016. http://www.nytimes.com/2016/02/24/opinion/campaign-stops/the-trump-sanders-fantasy.html

Egan, Timothy. 2016. "Lord of the Lies." *The New York Times,* June 9, 2016. https://www.nytimes.com/2016/06/10/opinion/lord-of-the-lies.html

Eilperin, Juliet. 2015. "Here's How the First President of the Social Media Age Has Chosen to Connect with Americans." *The Washington Post,* May 26, 2015. https://www.washingtonpost.com/news/politics/wp/2015/05/26/heres-how-the-first-president-of-the-social-media-age-has-chosen-to-connect-with-americans/?utm_term=.ad342d4ce720

Engel, Pamela. 2016. "Bernie Sanders Unloads on Hillary Clinton. 'I Don't Think You Are Qualified.'" *Business Insider,* April 7, 2016. http://www.businessinsider.com/bernie-sanders-hillary-clinton-unqualified-2016–4

Entous, Adam, Ellen Nakashima, and Greg Miller. 2016. "Secret CIA Assessment Says Russia Was Trying to Help Trump Win the White House." *The Washington Post,* December 9, 2016. https://www.washingtonpost.com/world/national-security/obama-orders-review-of-russian-hacking-during-presidential-campaign/2016/12/09/31d6b300-be2a-11e6-94ac-3d324840106c_story.html?utm_term=.837f1c51af8a

Erickson, Amanda. 2017. "The U.S. Is No Longer a 'Full Democracy,' a New Study Warns." *The Washington Post,* January 26, 2017. https://www.washingtonpost.com/news/worldviews/wp/2017/01/26/america-is-no-longer-a-full-democracy-a-new-study-warns/?utm_term=.c1e14cbf9cf2

Fagen, Sara. 2016. "Trump, Sanders: More Alike Than You Think" *CNBC,* March 11, 2016. http://www.cnbc.com/2016/03/11/trump-sanders-more-alike-than-you-think-commentary.html

Filipovic, Jill. 2016. "The Revenge of the White Man." *Time,* November 10, 2016. https://qz.com/1068114/googles-most-searched-how-to-questions-capture-all-the-magic-and-struggle-of-being-human/

Fitzpatrick, Meagan. 2016. "U.S. Candidate Comparison: Donald Trump and Bernie Sanders Have More in Common Than You Think." *CBC News,* March 26, 2016. http://www.cbc.ca/news/world/trump-sanders-similarities-1.3506257

Flinders, Matthew. 2016. "The Problems with Democracy—Continuing the Conversation into a New Year." *Oxford University Press Blog,* January 3, 2016. http://blog.oup.com/2016/01/problems-with-democracy/

Foran, Clare. 2016a. "Bernie Sanders's Case Against Hillary Clinton." *The Atlantic,* February 23, 2016. https://www.theatlantic.com/politics/archive/2016/02/bernie-sanders-hillary-clinton/470358/

———. 2016b. "The 'Never Clinton' Campaign." *The Atlantic,* May 5, 2016. http://www.theatlantic.com/politics/archive/2016/05/hillary-clinton-bernie-sanders/481389/

Frank, T.A. 2016. "Did Bernie Sanders Hand Trump the Election?" *Vanity Fair,* June 2016. https://www.vanityfair.com/news/2016/06/did-bernie-sanders-just-hand-trump-the-election

Fromm, Jeff. 2016. "New Study Finds Social Media Shapes Millennial Political Involvement and Engagement." *Forbes,* June 22, 2016. https://www.forbes.com/sites/jeff-fromm/2016/06/22/new-study-finds-social-media-shapes-millennial-political-involvement-and-engagement/#29d9f16d2618

Geiger, Matthew. 2016. "Decision 2016: Voter Choice is More Than Anti-Establishment." *Communities Digital News,* February 29, 2016. http://www.commdiginews.com/politics-2/election-2016/decision-2016-voter-choice-is-more-than-anti-establishment-58609/

Gerson, Michael. 2016. "Sanders's and Trump's Backward-Looking Plans Won't Help the Working Class." *The Washington Post,* March 21, 2016. https://www.washingtonpost.com/opinions/sanderss-and-trumps-backward-looking-plans-wont-help-the-working-class/2016/03/21/7aa119d2-ef8f-11e5-85a6-2132cf446d0a_story.html?utm_term=.dd4e84f7f5cc

———. 2017. "President Trump's 'Rhetorical Schizophrenia' is Easy to See Through." *The Washington Post,* August 28, 2017. https://www.washingtonpost.com/opinions/trumps-rhetorical-schizophrenia-is-easy-to-see-through/2017/08/24/2163ab42-88f3-11e7-a50f-e0d4e6ec070a_story.html?utm_term=.b57a7684838c

Gitlin, Todd. 2017. "Death by a Thousand Cut-and-Paste Jobs." *Moyers & Company,* April 14, 2017. http://billmoyers.com/story/death-thousand-cut-paste-jobs/

Gjelten, Tom. 2016. "Pew Report Tracks How Politics Correspond with Religion." *NPR,* July 13, 2016. http://www.npr.org/2016/07/13/485895807/pew-report-tracks-how-politics-correspond-with-religion

Goddard, Taegan. 2017. "Some Voters Tipped the Election to Trump." *Political Wire,* August 23, 2017. https://politicalwire.com/2017/08/23/sanders-voters-tipped-election-trump/

Goldberg, Jonah. 2017. "With President Trump the Abnormal is the New Normal." *Newsday,* August 23, 2017. http://www.newsday.com/opinion/commentary/with-president-trump-the-abnormal-is-the-new-normal-1.14085082

Goldberg, J.J. 2015. "Are Bernie Sanders and Donald Trump Flip Sides of Same Populist Coin?" *Forward,* September 2, 2015. http://forward.com/opinion/320261/are-bernie-sanders-and-donald-trump-opposite-sides-of-same-populist-coin/

"GOP: How Trump Defied All Predictions and Won." 2016. *The Week,* May 20, 2016. 18.

Graber, Doris. 1994. *Media Power in Politics.* Washington, D.C.: CQ Press.

Graham, David. 2017. "An Intelligence Report That Will Change No One's Mind." *The Atlantic,* January 6, 2017. https://www.theatlantic.com/politics/archive/2017/01/odni-report-on-russian-hacking/512465/

Gray, Chris. 2002. *Cyborg Citizens: Politics in the Posthuman Age.* New York: Routledge.

Gronbeck, Bruce E. 2004. "Citizen Voices in Cyberpolitical Culture." In *Rhetorical Democracy: Discursive Practices of Civic Engagement,* edited by Gerald Hauser and Amy Grim, 17–31. Mahwah, Lawrence Erlbaum Associates.

Grunwald, Michael. 2016. "Do Ideas Still Matter in the Year of Trump (and Clinton)?" *Politico,* September / October 2016. http://www.politico.com/magazine/story/2016/09/2016-policy-ideas-hillary-clinton-donald-trump-future-214222

Halpern, Sue. 2017. "How He Used Facebook to Win." *The New York Review of Books,* June 8, 2017.

Hamilton, Alexander, James Madison, and John Jay. 1787, 2014. *The Federalist: A Collection of Essays, Written in Favor of the New Constitution, As Agreed Upon by the Federal Convention.* Mineola: Dover Publications.

Healy, Patrick. 2016a. "As Hillary Clinton Sweeps States, One Group Resists: White Men." *The New York Times,* March 17, 2016. https://www.nytimes.com/2016/03/18/us/politics/as-hillary-clinton-sweeps-states-one-group-resists-white-men.html?_r=2

———. 2016b. "'Brexit' Revolt Cast a Shadow Over Clinton's Cautious Path." *The New York Times,* June 10, 2016. http://www.nytimes.com/2016/06/26/us/politics/brexit-revolt-casts-a-shadow-over-hillary-clintons-caution.html?smid=fb-nytimes&smtyp=cur&mtrref=l.facebook.com&gwh=4F7E23F343595F5F519C74167939AD26&gwt=pay

Ho, Katherine. 2016. "Letter to the Editor." *The New York Times,* June 29, 2016. http://www.nytimes.com/2016/06/30/opinion/dear-bernie-sanders-what-you-didnt-say.html?smid=fb-share

Hochschild, Jennifer L. 2010. "If Democracies Need Informed Voters, How Can They Thrive While Expanding Enfranchisement?" *Election Law Journal: Rules, Politics, and Policy* 9, no: 2 (June 2010): 111–123. https://scholar.harvard.edu/jlhochschild/publications/if-democracies-need-informed-voters-how-can-they-thrive-while-expanding-en

Hohmann, James. 2016. "The Daily 202: Liberal Allies Turning on Bernie Sanders after Nevada Donnybrook." *The Washington Post,* May 18, 2016. https://www.washingtonpost.com/news/powerpost/paloma/daily-202/2016/05/18/daily-202-liberal-allies-turning-on-bernie-sanders-after-nevada-donnybrook/573b56ed981b92a22d86b9d2/?utm_term=.3606f4275ddc

Holan, Angie and Linda Qiu. 2015. "2015 Lie of the Year: The Campaign Misstatements of Donald Trump." *Politifact,* December 21, 2015. http://www.politifact.com/truth-o-meter/article/2015/dec/21/2015-lie-year-donald-trump-campaign-misstatements/

"Illiteracy Statistics." 2016. *Statistic Brain,* August 22, 2016. http://www.statisticbrain.com/number-of-american-adults-who-cant-read/

Iyengar, Shanto and Donald Kinder. 1987, 2010. *News That Matters: Television and American Opinion.* Chicago: University of Chicago Press.

Jackson, David. 2016. "Bush Ran Aground Over Trump Anti-Establishment Policies." *USA Today,* February 22, 2016. http://www.usatoday.com/story/news/2016/02/21/jeb-bush-donald-trump-republicans-2016/80702192/

Janack, James A. 2006. "The Rhetoric of 'The Body:' Jesse Ventura and Bakhtin's Carnival." *Communication Studies* 57, no. 2 (August 21, 2006): 197–214.

Jerde, Sara. 2016. "Pence as VP: He's a Solid Person." *TPM,* July 16, 2016. http://talkingpointsmemo.com/livewire/trump-introduces-pence-vp-pick

Johnson, Ted. 2016. "Lena Dunham Says She Has Received 'More Hostility' for Backing Clinton Over Sanders." *Variety,* March 20, 2016. http://variety.com/2016/biz/news/lena-dunham-hillary-clinton-bernie-sanders-1201734952/

Jones, Robert. 2016. "How Trump Remixed the Republican 'Southern Strategy.'" *The Republic,* August 14, 2016. https://www.theatlantic.com/politics/archive/2016/08/how-trump-remixed-the-republican-southern-strategy/495719/

Jones, Sarah. 2016. "Republican Official Warns That Supporting Trump is Smearing the GOP With Excrement." *Politicususa,* July 3, 2016. http://www.politicususa.com/2016/07/03/gop-strategist-warns-supporting-trump-smearing-gop-reek-excreta-decades.html

Kakutani, Michiko. 2017. "'Shattered' Charts Hillary Clinton's Course Into the Iceberg." *The New York Times,* April 17, 2017. https://www.nytimes.com/2017/04/17/books/shattered-charts-hillary-clintons-course-into-the-iceberg.html?_r=0&mtrref=undefined&mtrref=www.nytimes.com&mtrref=www.nytimes.com&gwh=F5080370936265806D7BC6CADCE534C8&gwt=pay

Kazin, Michael. 2016. "How Can Bernie Sanders and Donald Trump Both Be 'Populist?'" *The New York Times Magazine,* March 22, 2016. https://www.nytimes.com/

2016/03/27/magazine/how-can-donald-trump-and-bernie-sanders-both-be-populist.html?mcubz=3&_r=0

Keane, John. 2016. "Donald Trump Is an Existential Threat to American Democracy." *The Drum*, March 13, 2016. http://www.abc.net.au/news/2016–03–14/keane-trump-is-an-existential-threat-to-american-democracy/7244240

Keith, Tamara. 2016. "Research Challenges Assumptions on Why Voters Support Trump." *NPR*, August 22, 2016. http://www.npr.org/2016/08/22/490895567/research-challenges-assumptions-on-why-voters-support-trump

Kelemen, R. Daniel. 2016. "A Dark Age for European Democracy?" *Foreign Affairs*, December 7, 2016. https://www.foreignaffairs.com/articles/europe/2016–12–07/dark-age-european-democracy

Kelley, Colleen. 2007. *Post-911 American Presidential Rhetoric: A Study of Protofascist Discourse*. Lanham: Lexington Books.

Kelley, J-D. (3 March 2016). Response to *The Wall Street Journal's* graphic compilation 'How Trump Happened.' http://graphics.wsj.com/elections/2016/how-trump-happened/. Personal Interview.

Kelly, Mary, and Emma Bowman. 2016. "CIA Concludes Russian Interference Aimed to Elect Trump." *NPR*, December 10, 2016. http://www.npr.org/sections/thetwo-way/2016/12/10/505072304/cia-concludes-russian-interference-aimed-to-elect-trump

Kendall-Taylor, Andrea and Erica Frantz. 2016. "How Democracies Fall Apart: Why Populism is a Pathway to Autocracy." *Foreign Affairs*, December 5, 2016. https://www.foreignaffairs.com/articles/2016–12–05/how-democracies-fall-apart

Kernell, Samuel, and Gary Jacobson. 1987. "Congress and the Presidency as News in the 19th Century." *The Journal of Politics* 49, no. 4 (November 1987): 1016–1035.

Kerr, Jennifer. 2016. "Trump Overwhelmingly Leads Rivals in Support from Less Educated Americans." *PBS*, April 3, 2016. http://www.pbs.org/newshour/rundown/trump-overwhelmingly-leads-rivals-in-support-from-less-educated-americans/

Kiely, Eugene. 2017. "Trump Misleads on Russia Hacking." *FactCheck.org*, July 7, 2017. http://www.factcheck.org/2017/07/trump-misleads-russia-hacking/

Kilgore, Ed. 2016. "Sanders Needs to Talk Down His Supporters and Explain That Nothing is Being 'Stolen.'" *New York Magazine*, May 18, 2016. http://nymag.com/daily/intelligencer/2016/05/sanders-needs-to-talk-down-his-supporters.html

King, Jr., Neil. 2016. "Hillary Clinton. v. Donald Trump: A Look at the Numbers." *The Wall Street Journal*, June 9, 2016. http://blogs.wsj.com/washwire/2016/06/09/hillary-clinton-v-donald-trump-a-look-at-the-numbers/

Kinzel, Bob. 2015. "Bernie Sanders Uses Social Media to Bypass Mainstream Outlets." *VPR News*, July 10, 2015. http://digital.vpr.net/post/bernie-sanders-uses-social-media-bypass-mainstream-outlets#stream/0

Kirsch, Irwin S., Ann Jungeblut, Lynn Jenkins, and Andrew Kolstad. 2002. *Adult Literacy in America*. 3rd ed. Washington, D.C.: National Center for Education Statistics.

Klein, Ezra. 2016. "Understanding Hillary: Why the Clinton America Sees Isn't the Clinton Colleagues Know." *VOX*, July 11, 2016. https://www.vox.com/a/hillary-clinton-interview/the-gap-listener-leadership-quality

———. 2017. "Here's the Real Reason Hillary Lost the Election." *CNBC*, June 2, 2017. https://www.cnbc.com/2017/06/02/why-im-defending-hillary-clinton-commentary.html

Kolbert, Elizabeth. 2017. "Why Facts Don't Change Our Minds." *The New Yorker*, February 27, 2017. https://www.newyorker.com/magazine/2017/02/27/why-facts-dont-change-our-minds

Konnikova, Maria. 2017. "Trump's Lies vs. Your Brain." *Politico*, January / February 2017. http://www.politico.com/magazine/story/2017/01/donald-trump-lies-liar-effect-brain-214658

Korade, Matt, and Eli Watkins. 2017. "Trump: Hillary Clinton and Democratic Party 'Colluded' Against Sanders." *CNN*, June 25, 2017. http://www.cnn.com/2017/06/25/politics/trump-tweet-hillary-collusion/index.html

Kosinski, Michelle, and Nicole Gaouette. 2017. "Despite Frustration, Tillerson Says Trump Relationship is 'Good.'" *CNN*, July 27, 2017. http://www.cnn.com/2017/07/26/politics/tillerson-turmoil-trump-tweets/index.html

Kreiss, Daniel. 2016. *Prototype Politics: Technology-Intensive Campaigning and the Data of Democracy.* New York: Oxford University Press.

Kristof, Nicholas. 2016. "Is Donald Trump a Racist?" *The New York Times,* July 23, 2016. https://www.nytimes.com/2016/07/24/opinion/sunday/is-donald-trump-a-racist.html

Kruger, Jason and David Dunning. 1999. "Unskilled and Unaware of It: How Difficulties in Recognizing One's Own Incompetence Lead to Inflated Self-Assessments." *Journal of Personality and Social Psychology* 77, no. 6 (1999): 1121–1134. http://www.jerwood-no.org.uk/pdf/Dunning%20Kruger.pdf

Krugman, Paul. 2016a. "How America Was Lost." *The New York Times,* February 14, 2016. http://www.nytimes.com/2016/02/15/opinion/how-america-was-lost.html?_r=0

———. 2016b. "Varieties of Voodoo." *The New York Times,* February 19, 2016. http://www.nytimes.com/2016/02/19/opinion/varieties-of-voodoo.html?_r=0

———. 2016c. "Sanders Over the Edge." *The New York Times,* April 8, 2016. http://www.nytimes.com/2016/04/08/opinion/sanders-over-the-edge.html?smid=fb-nytimes&smtyp=cur&_r=0

———. 2016d. "Hillary and the Horizontals." *The New York Times,* June 10, 2016. https://www.nytimes.com/2016/06/10/opinion/hillary-and-the-horizontals.html?_r=1

———. 2016e. "The Tainted Election." *The New York Times,* December 12, 2016. https://www.nytimes.com/2016/12/12/opinion/the-tainted- election.html

Kurtzleben, Danielle. 2017. "Here's How Many Bernie Sanders Supporters Ultimately Voted for Trump." *NPR,* August 24, 2017. http://www.newsweek.com/bernie-sanders-trump-2016-election-654320

Latifi, Veton. 2015. "The Populism of Political Discourse: Metamorphoses of Political Rhetoric and Populism." *South-East European Journal of Political Science* 4, no. 2 (June-December 2015): (2). http://seejps.lumina.org/index.php/volume-ii-number-1–2-populism-and-its-metamorphoses/71-the-populism-of-the-political-discourse-metamorphoses-of-political-rhetoric-and-populism

Leibovich, Mark. 2016. "The Decorous Demise of the 'Establishment.'" *The New York Times,* March 1, 2016. http://www.nytimes.com/2016/03/06/magazine/the-decorous-demise-of-the-establishment.html?rref= collection%2Ftimestopic%2FBush%2C%20Jeb&action=click&contentCollection= timestopics&region=stream&module=stream_unit&version=latest& contentPlacement=5&pgtype=collection

Le Miere, Jason. 2017. "Bernie Sanders Voters Helped Trump Win and Here's Proof." *Newsweek,* August 23, 2017. http://www.newsweek.com/bernie-sanders-trump-2016-election-654320

Lepore, Jill. 2016. "The Party Crashers: Is the New Populism About the Medium or the Message?" *The New Yorker,* February 22, 2016. https://www.newyorker.com/magazine/2016/02/22/did-social-media-produce-the-new-populism

Lightner, Diana. 2016. "Revoke Bernie Sanders's Membership in the Democratic Party." *Change.org,* June 15, 2016. https://www.change.org/p/democratic-national-committee-revoke-bernie-sander-s-membership-in-the-democratic-party

Lipton, Eric, David Sanger, and Scott Shane. 2016. "The Perfect Weapon: How Russian Cyberpower Invaded the U.S." *The New York Times,* December 13, 2016. https://www.nytimes.com/2016/12/13/us/politics/russia-hack-election-dnc.html?_r=0

Long, Ray. 2016. "Why Did Hillary Clinton Lose? Simple. She Ran a Bad Campaign." *Chicago Tribune,* November 14, 2016. http://www.chicagotribune.com/news/opinion/commentary/ct-hillary-clinton-lost-bad-campaign-perspec-20161114-story.html

Lowe, Josh. 2016. "Why the 'Poorly Educated' Love Donald Trump Back." *Newsweek,* November 25, 2016. http://www.newsweek.com/donald-trump-brexit-austria-french-presidential-election-national-front-525281

Luhby, Tami. 2016. "Here are the Massive Tax Breaks Trump is Proposing for the Rich." *CNN Money,* May 9, 2016. http://money.cnn.com/2016/05/09/news/economy/trump-tax-rich/index.html

Lukianoff, Greg, and Jonathan Haidt. 2015. "The Coddling of the American Mind." *The Atlantic,* September 2015. https://www.theatlantic.com/magazine/archive/2015/09/the-coddling-of-the-american-mind/399356/

Madden, Heather. 2015. "The Outsiders: Public Discontent and a New Class of Presidential Hopefuls." *The American Spectator,* September 28, 2015. http://www.iwvoice.org/detail.php?c=2798293&t=THE-OUTSIDERS%3A-Public-discontent-and-a-new-class-of-Presidential-hopefuls

Mahbubani, Kishore. 2016. "Why Asia Doesn't Have a Donald Trump or Bernie Sanders." *The Huffington Post,* February 24, 2016. http://www.huffingtonpost.com/kishore-mahbubani/asia-trump-sanders-populism_b_9299086.html

Marchant, Bristow. 2016. "Is Trump a Fascist? Winthrop History Professor Weighs In." *The Herald,* February 5, 2016. http://www.heraldonline.com/news/local/article58699793.html

Marche, Stephen. 2016. "The White Man Pathology: Inside the Fandom of Sanders and Trump." *The Guardian,* January 10, 2016. https://www.theguardian.com/us-news/2016/jan/10/white-man-pathology-bernie-sanders-donald-trump?CMP=share_btn_fb

McLuhan, Marshall. 1964. *Understanding Media: The Extensions of Man.* New York: McGraw-Hill.

McNeill, John. 2016. "How Fascist is Donald Trump? There's Actually a Formula for That." *The Washington Post,* October 21, 2016. https://www.washingtonpost.com/posteverything/wp/2016/10/21/how-fascist-is-donald-trump-theres-actually-a-formula-for-that/?utm_term=.9a9bf3594a72

Mead, Walter Russell. 2017. "The Jacksonian Revolt." *Hudson Institute,* January 20, 2017. https://www.hudson.org/research/13258-the-jacksonian-revolt

Medhurst, Martin. 2004. *Beyond the Rhetorical Presidency.* College Station: Texas A&M University Press.

Mercieca, Jennifer. 2015. "The Rhetorical Brilliance of Trump the Demagogue." *The Huffington Post,* December 12, 2015. http://www.huffingtonpost.com/the-conversation-us/the-rhetorical-brilliance_b_8792452.html

———. 2016. "How Donald Trump Gets Away With Saying Things Other Candidates Can't." *Raw Story,* March 8, 2016. http://www.rawstory.com/2016/03/how-donald-trump-gets-away-with-saying-things-other-candidates-cant/

Mickey, Robert, Steven Levitsky, and Lucan Ahmad Way. 2017. "Is America Still Safe for Democracy? Why the United States is in Danger of Backsliding." *Foreign Affairs,* May 2017. http://cf.linnbenton.edu/artcom/social_science/clarkd/upload/Is%20America%20Still%20Safe%20for%20Democracy.pdf

"Millennial Impact Report: Waves 1, 2, and 3 and Post Election Survey." 2016. *The Case Foundation.* https://casefoundation.org/resource/millennial-impact-report-2016/

Millward, David. 2016. "Donald Trump Pulls Out of Debate with Bernie Sanders, Saying it Would Be 'Inappropriate.'" *The Telegraph News,* May 28, 2016. http://www.telegraph.co.uk/news/2016/05/28/donald-trump-pulls-out-of-debate-with-bernie-sanders-saying-it-w/

Modhin, Aamna. 2016. "American Women Voted Overwhelmingly for Clinton, Except the White Ones." *Quartz Media,* November 9, 2016. https://qz.com/1068114/googles-most-searched-how-to-questions-capture-all-the-magic-and-struggle-of-being-human/

Montanaro, Domenco. 2016. "7 Reasons Donald Trump Won the Presidential Election." *NPR,* November 12, 2016. http://www.npr.org/2016/11/12/501848636/7-reasons-donald-trump-won-the-presidential-election

Mortensen, Mette. 2017. *Journalism and Eyewitness Images: Digital Media, Participation, and Conflict*. London: Routledge.

Morton, Phillip. 2016. "Bernie Sanders: Winning Personality." *The Huffington Post*, October 9, 2016. http://www.huffingtonpost.com/philip-morton/bernie-sanders-winning-pe_b_8272156.html

Moyer, Justin. 2016. "Trump's Grammar in Speeches 'Just Below 6th Grade Level,' Study Finds." *The Washington Post*, March 18, 2016. https://www.washingtonpost.com/news/morning-mix/wp/2016/03/18/trumps-grammar-in-speeches-just-below-6th-grade-level-study-finds/

Mulholland, Bob. 2016. "Super Delegate Bob Mulholland Writes a Blistering Open Letter to Bernie Sanders." *Democratic Underground*, April 6, 2016. http://www.democraticunderground.com/110798504

Natale, Darlene. 2016. "From Hope and Change to Anger and Anxiety: Demagoguery and Discourse in the 2016 Primary Elections." Paper presented at the *National Communication Association Annual Meeting [Philadelphia, PA]*, November 2016.

Nevius, James. 2016. "The Loose-Cannon Candidate May be the New Normal." *The Guardian*, May 13, 2016. https://www.theguardian.com/commentisfree/2016/may/12/bernie-sanders-donald-trump-divisive-personality-politics

O'Malley, Martin and Peter Levin. 2017. "How To Counter Fake News: Technology Can Help Distinguish Facts From Fiction." *Foreign Affairs*, January 5, 2017. https://www.foreignaffairs.com/articles/americas/2017-01-05/how-counter-fake-news

Oswald, Kristine. 2009. "Mass Media and the Transformation of American Politics." *Marquette University Law Review* 77, no. 2 (2009): 385–414.

Parker, Ashley, and Jonathan Martin. 2016. "Donald Trump Borrows From Bernie Sanders's Playbook To Woo Democrats." *The New York Times*, May 17, 2016. http://www.nytimes.com/2016/05/18/us/politics/donald-trump-bernie-sanders-campaign.html?_r=0

Parry-Giles, Trevor. 2016. "Pop Culture and the Presidency." *Spectra* 52, no. 3 & 4 (September / November 2016): 40–45.

Pasley, Jeffrey. 2003. "The Role of the Press and Media in American Presidential Elections." In *American Presidential Campaigns and Elections*, edited by William G. Shed, Ballard Campbell, and Craig Coenen. New York: M.E. Sharpe.

Patterson, James. 2016. "The Literacy of Long-Form Thinking." *Time*, October 13, 2016. http://time.com/collection-post/4521571/2016-election-james-patterson/

Patterson, Thomas E. 2016a. "Pre-Primary News Coverage of the 2016 Presidential Race: Trump's Rise, Sanders's Emergence, Clinton's Struggle." *Harvard Kennedy School Shorenstein Center on Media, Politics and Public Policy*, June 13, 2016. http://shorensteincenter.org/pre-primary-news-coverage-2016-trump-clinton-sanders/

———. 2016b. "New Coverage of the 2016 Presidential Primaries: Horse Race Reporting Has Consequences." *Harvard Kennedy School Shorenstein Center on Media, Politics and Public Policy*, July 11, 2016. http://shorensteincenter.org/news-coverage-2016-presidential-primaries/

Paxton, Robert O. 1998. "The Five Stages of Fascism." *The Journal of Modern History* 70, no. 1 (March 1998): 1–23.

Pazienza, Chez. 2016. "Bernie vs. Trump: The Batsh*t Political Fringes Finally Come Together. *The Daily Banter*, May 26, 2016. http://thedailybanter.com/2016/05/trump-sanders-debate/

Peters, Jeremy. 2017. "In Free-Range Trump, Many See Potential for a Third Party." *The New York Times*, September 11, 2017. https://www.nytimes.com/2017/09/11/us/politics/trump-third-party-republican.html?_r=0

Peters, Jeremy, and Alan Rappeport. "Bernie Sanders's Defiance Strains Ties with Top Democrats." *Tampa Bay Times*, May 18, 2016. http://www.tampabay.com/news/politics/national/sanders-defiance-strains-ties-with-top-democrats-wvideo/2277980

Pillar, Paul. 2016. "Trump's Blatantly Racist Campaign." *Consortium News*, June 16, 2016. https://consortiumnews.com/2016/06/16/trumps-blatantly-racist-campaign/

Pitts, Jr., Leonard. 2016. "Sanders' Supporters Are Content to Lose Both the Battle and the War." *Miami Herald,* April 29, 2016. http://www.miamiherald.com/opinion/opn-columns-blogs/leonard-pitts-jr/article74777987.html

Plato. 1871, 2005. *The Republic.* Translated by Benjamin Jowett. New York: Barnes and Noble. "Political Processes and Television." 2017. *Museum of Broadcast Communications.* http://www.museum.tv/eotv/politicalpro.htm

"Political Processes and Television." 2017 *Museum of Broadcast Communications.* http://www.museum.tv/eotv/politicalpro.htm.

Poniewozik, James. 2017. "Review: 'American Horror Story: Cult' Feeds Off Trump-Era Fears." *The New York Times,* September 4, 2017. https://www.nytimes.com/2017/09/04/arts/television/american-horror-story-cult-review.html

Pottle, Lydia. 1999. "The Work of Art in the Age of Digital Reproduction." *University of Pennsylvania,* April 28, 1999. https://www.stwing.upenn.edu/~lpottle/RabateFinal.html

Poundstone, William. 2017. "The Dunning-Kruger President." *Psychology Today,* January 21, 2017. https://www.psychologytoday.com/blog/head-in-the-cloud/201701/the-dunning-kruger-president

"Presidential Candidates' Changing Relationship with the Web." 2016. *Pew Research Center.* July 18, 2016. http://www.journalism.org/2016/07/18/presidential-candidates-changing-relationship-with-the-web/.

Ranney, Austin. 1984. *Channels of Power: The Impact of Television on American Politics.* New York: Basic Books.

Rappeport, Alan. 2015. "Bernie Sanders, Long Serving Independent, Enters Presidential Race as a Democrat." *The New York Times,* April 29, 2015.

———. 2016. "From Bernie Sanders Supporters: Death Threats Over Delegates." *The New York Times,* May 16, 2016. http://www.nytimes.com/2016/05/17/us/politics/bernie-sanders-supporters-nevada.html?smprod=nytcore-iphone&smid=nytcore-iphone-'share

Rauch, Jonathan. 2015. "Amateurs in the Oval Office: Why Americans Tend More and More to Want Inexperienced Candidates." *The Atlantic,* November 2015. https://www.theatlantic.com/magazine/archive/2015/11/amateurs-in-the-oval-office/407830/

"Research: Media Coverage of the 2016 Election." 2016. *Harvard Kennedy School's Shorenstein Center on Media, Politics, and Public Policy,* September 7, 2016. https://shorensteincenter.org/research-media-coverage-2016-election/

Reston, Maeve. 2016. "Bernie Sanders Pledges to Stay in Race. *CNN,* June 8, 2016. http://www.cnn.com/2016/06/08/politics/bernie-sanders-2016-election/index.html

Rhodan, Maya. 2017. "President Trump Still Attacking Hillary Clinton 5 Months After the Election." *Time,* April 3, 2017. http://www.foxnews.com/politics/2017/07/25/trump-vs-clinton-feud-continues-even-after-election.html

Robbins, Mel. 2016. "The Trump Tape Doesn't Matter." *CNN,* October 10, 2016. http://www.cnn.com/2016/10/09/opinions/trump-tape-doesnt-matter-opinion-robbins/index.html

Roberts, Cokie and Steve Roberts. 2016a. "Reckless Promises Plaguing U.S. Politics." *Erie Times News,* February 19, 2016. http://www.goerie.com/news/20160219/reckless-promises-plaguing-us-politics-cokie-and-steve-roberts

———. 2016b. "Parties Would Derail Trump, Sanders at their Peril." *GoErie.com,* March 11, 2016. http://www.goerie.com/news/20160311/parties-would-derail-trump-sanders-at-their-peril-cokie-and-steve-roberts

Rohac, Dailbor and Jan Zilinsky. 2015. "Beware Populist Snake Oil." *U.S. News and World Report,* September 24, 2015. http://www.worldpoliticsreview.com/trend-lines/20427/donald-trump-and-the-global-rise-of-populism

Rolfe, Mark. 2016. *The Reinvention of Populist Rhetoric in the Digital Age: Insiders and Outsiders in Democratic Politics.* New York: Macmillan.

Rosario, Justin. 2016. "Civil Rights Legend Tom Hayden Abandons Bernie for Hillary." *Left Wing Nation*, April 13, 2016. http://leftwingnation.org/civil-rights-legend-tom-hayden-abandons-bernie-for-hillary/

Rosenstiel, Tom, Amy Mitchell, Kristen Purcell, and Lee Rainie. 2011. "Part 3: The Role of Newspapers." *Pew Research Center*, September 26, 2011. http://www.pewinternet.org/2011/09/26/part-3-the-role-of-newspapers/

Ross, Janell. 2015. "Just How Unique is the Political Rhetoric of the Donald Trump Era?" *The Washington Post*, December 7, 2015. https://www.washingtonpost.com/news/the-fix/wp/2015/12/07/is-our-out-of-control-political-rhetoric-really-all-that-extraordinary/

"Running for President." 2016. *The Presidents*. American Experience. PBS. http://www.pbs.org/wgbh/americanexperience/features/presidents/

Samoilenko, Sergei. 2016. "Character Assassination." In *The SAGE Encyclopedia of Corporate Reputation*, edited by Craig E. Carroll, 116–118. Thousand Oaks: SAGE Publications. doi: 10.4135/9781483376493.n52.

Samuelson, Robert J. 2016. "Why You Might Just Miss Old-Time Political Bosses." *The Washington Post*, March 6, 2016. https://www.washingtonpost.com/opinions/why-you-might-just-miss-old-time-political-bosses/2016/03/06/d6494f7e-e22a-11e5-8d98-4b3d9215ade1_story.html?utm_term=.a9cf3a36de97

Sanders, Bernie. 2015a. "Transcript of the Bernard Sanders 2016 Presidential Announcement Speech." *Irregular Times*, April 20, 2015. http://irregulartimes.com/2015/04/30/transcript-of-the-bernard-sanders-2016-presidential-announcement-speech/

———. 2015b. "Bernie's Announcement: Bernie Sanders Announces Bid for Democratic Presidential Nomination." *BernieSanders.com*, May 26, 2015. https://berniesanders.com/bernies-announcement/

———. 2015c. "In 180 Seconds You Will Be Voting for Bernie Sanders." *YouTube*, August 2, 2015. https://www.youtube.com/watch?v=RGMc032rrj0

———. 2016a. "Full Transcript: CNN Democratic Debate." *CNN*, April 15, 2016. http://www.cnn.com/2016/04/14/politics/transcript-democratic-debate-hillary-clinton-bernie-sanders/index.html

———. 2016b. "Transcript: Bernie Sanders Speech in Burlington, Vermont." *Politico*, June 16, 2016. http://www.politico.com/story/2016/06/transcript-bernie-sanders-speech-in-burlington-vermont-224465

———. 2016c. "Prepared Remarks: Portsmouth Organizing Event with Bernie Sanders and Hillary Clinton." *BernieSanders.com*, July 12, 2016. https://berniesanders.com/prepared-remarks-bernie-clinton/?source=pressrelease

———. 2016d. "Transcript: Bernie Sanders Full Speech at the 2016 DNC." *The Washington Post*, July 26, 2016. https://www.washingtonpost.com/news/post-politics/wp/2016/07/26/transcript-bernie-sanderss-full-speech-at-the-2016-dnc/

Sanger, David, and Scott Shane. 2016. "Russian Hackers Acted to Aid Russia in Election, US Says." *The New York Times*, December 9, 2016. https://www.theatlantic.com/politics/archive/2017/01/odni-report-on-russian-hacking/512465/

Savel, Maria. 2016. "Donald Trump and the Global Rise of Populism." *World Politics Review*, November 10, 2016. http://www.worldpoliticsreview.com/trend-lines/20427/donald-trump-and-the-global-rise-of-populism

Schlueter, Nathan. 2016. "The Politics of Passion: A Lesson from the Federalist Papers." *Public Discourse*, February 25, 2016. http://www.thepublicdiscourse.com/2016/02/16524/

Seabrook. 2007. "Ron Paul, Glen Greenwald, and the Rhetoric of the 'Outsider.'" *Daily-Kos*, November 6, 2007. https://www.dailykos.com/stories/2007/11/6/407216/-

Seagrave, S. Adam. 2016. "What Trump and Sanders Teach Us About America." *Public Discourse*, March 23, 2016. http://www.thepublicdiscourse.com/2016/03/16629/

Seitz-Wald, Alex. 2016a. "Bernie Sanders Wins in Oregon, But He Needed Kentucky Too." *NBC News*, May 18, 2016. http://www.nbcnews.com/politics/2016-election/bernie-sanders-wins-oregon-he-needed-kentucky-too-n575846

———. 2016b. "How Bernie Sanders Supporters Shut Down a Donald Trump Rally in Chicago." *MSNBC*, March 12, 2016. http://www.msnbc.com/msnbc/how-bernie-sanders-supporters-shut-down-donald-trump-rally-chicago

———. 2016c. "'Bernie Mafia': Sanders Supporters Look to Seize Democratic Party Initiative." *NBC News*, November 21, 2016. https://www.nbcnews.com/politics/2016-election/bernie-mafia-sanders-supporters-look-seize-democratic-party-initiative-n686531

Selnow, Gary. 1998. *Electronic Whistle-Stops: The Impact of the Internet on American Politics*. Westport: Praeger.

Shane, Scott. 2017. "The Fake Americans Russia Created to Influence the Election." *The New York Times*, September 7, 2017. https://query.nytimes.com/search/sitesearch/?action=click&contentCollection&region=TopBar&WT.nav=searchWidget&module=SearchSubmit&pgtype=Homepage#/The Fake Americans Russia Created to Influence the Election

Shapiro, Ben. 2016. "Sanders and Trump Are the Same Totalitarian Candidate." *The Daily Wire*, February 10, 2016. http://www.dailywire.com/news/3280/sanders-and-trump-are-same-totalitarian-candidate-ben-shapiro

Shapiro, Stuart. 2015. "Trump is Latest in Long Line of Demagogues." *The Hill*, September 3, 2015. http://thehill.com/blogs/pundits-blog/presidential-campaign/252598-trump-is-latest-in-long-line-of-demagogues

Shepherd, Alex. 2016. "Donald Trump Loves the Poorly Educated." *The New Republic*, February 24, 2016. https://newrepublic.com/minutes/130419/donald-trump-loves-poorly-educated

Shiraev, Eric. 2010. "Character Assassination: An Interdisciplinary Approach." *George Mason University*, October 2010. https://characterattack.files.wordpress.com/2010/10/character-assassination-an-interdisciplinary-approach.pdf

Silver, Nate. 2016. "Was the Democratic Primary a Close Call or a Landslide?" *FiveThirtyEight*, July 27, 2016. http://fivethirtyeight.com/features/was-the-democratic-primary-a-close-call-or-a-landslide

———. 2017. "The Comey Letter Probably Cost Clinton the Election: So Why Won't the Media Admit as Much." *FiveThirtyEight*, May 3, 2017. https://fivethirtyeight.com/features/the-comey-letter-probably-cost-clinton-the-election/

Smith, Allison. 2016. "Donald Trump Speaks Like A Sixth-Grader." *The Washington Post*, May 3, 2016. https://www.washingtonpost.com/posteverything/wp/2016/05/03/donald-trump-speaks-like-a-sixth-grader-all-politicians-should/?utm_term=.5fa681c31f0c

Smith, Kristian Nicole. 2011. *Social Media and Political Campaigns*. Tennessee: University of Tennessee. http://trace.tennessee.edu/cgi/viewcontent.cgi?article=2442&context=utk_chanhonoproj

Somin, Ilya. 2004. "When Ignorance Isn't Bliss: How Political Ignorance Threatens Democracy." *CATO Institute*, September 22, 2004. http://www.cato.org/publications/policy-analysis/when-ignorance-isnt-bliss-how-political-ignorance-threatens-democracy

———. 2013. *Democracy and Political Ignorance*. Redwood City: Stanford University Press.

———. 2016. "Political Ignorance Haunts 2016 Campaign." *CNN.com*, May 12, 2016. http://www.cnn.com/2016/05/12/opinions/political-ignorance-somin/index.html

Stanley, Jason. 2015. "Democracy and the Demagogue." *The New York Times*, October 12, 2015. http://opinionator.blogs.nytimes.com/2015/10/12/democracy-and-the-demagogue/

Steinhorn, Leonard. 2017. "Donald Trump's Populism Decoded: How a Billionaire Became the Voice of the 'Little People.'" *Moyers and Company*, July 3, 2017. http://billmoyers.com/story/donald-trumps-populism-decoded-billionaire-became-voice-little-people/

Stevenson, Peter. 2016. "Donald Trump Loves the 'Poorly Educated'—And Just About Everyone Else in Nevada." *The Washington Post*, February 24, 2016. https://

www.washingtonpost.com/news/the-fix/wp/2016/02/24/donald-trump-loves-the-poorly-educated-and-just-about-everyone-else-in-nevada/?utm_term=.11bfec84f978

Stid, Daniel. 2014. "We're All Amateurs Now." *Hewlett Foundation,* July 30, 2014. http://www.hewlett.org/were-all-amateurs-now/

Stockdell-Giesler, Anne Meade. 2010. *Agency in the Margins: Stories of Outsider Rhetoric.* Madison: Fairleigh Dickinson University.

Stuckey, Mary. 2010. "'The Joshua Generation': Rethinking the Rhetorical Presidency and Presidential Rhetoric." *ScholarWorks at Georgia State University,* 2010. http://scholarworks.gsu.edu/cgi/viewcontent.cgi?article=1018&context=communication_facpub

———. 2016. "Stability and Change in the Rhetoric of the 2016 Presidential Primaries." *Spectra* 52, no. 3&4 (September / November 2016): 10–16.

Sullivan, Andrew. 2016. "Democracies End When They Are Too Democratic: And Right Now, America is a Breeding Ground for Tyranny." *New York Magazine,* May 1, 2016. http://nymag.com/daily/intelligencer/2016/04/america-tyranny-donald-trump.html

Sullivan, Sean and Mike DeBonis. 2017. "Lawmakers Say Trump's Words Matter—And Hurt the Country's Standing Abroad." *The Washington Post,* February 18, 2017. https://www.washingtonpost.com/powerpost/lawmakers-say-trumps-words-matter--and-are-hurting-the-countrys-standing-abroad/2017/02/17/1cacaa9e-f55b-11e6-a9b0-ecee7ce475fc_story.html?utm_term=.34b3d71ce4c1

Swanson, Ana. 2017. "Analysis: The Rise of Populism Should Not Have Surprised Anyone." *SentinelSource.com,* August 13, 2017. http://www.sentinelsource.com/news/national_world/analysis-the-rise-of-populism-shouldn-t-have-surprised-anyone/article_df73b26a-5cce-536c-8866-763c53af4a00.html

Tani, Maxell. 2016a. "TRUMP: I'm Going to be Borrowing Some of Bernie's 'Material' Against Hillary." *Business Insider,* April 27, 2016.http://www.businessinsider.com/trump-bernie-hillary-election-2016-4

———. 2016b. "Bernie Sanders is Escalating His Attacks on Clinton—And Trump is Taking Notes." *Business Insider,* May 2, 2016. http://www.businessinsider.com/bernie-sanders-hillary-clinton-indiana-polls-attacks-2016-5

———. 2017. "When Asked If the President Represents American Values, Rex Tillerson Says Trump 'Speaks for Himself.'" *Business Insider,* August 27, 2017. http://www.businessinsider.com/tillerson-trump-speaks for himself-fox-news-sunday-2017-8

Taub, Amanda. 2016. "The Rise of American Authoritarianism." *VOX,* March 1, 2016. https://www.vox.com/2016/3/1/11127424/trump-authoritarianism

Terkel, Amanda. 2016a. "Sorry Brown People, Donald Trump Doesn't Believe You're Real Americans." *The Huffington Post,* June 2, 2016. http://www.huffingtonpost.com/entry/donald-trump-mexicans_us_5751e972e4b0c3752dcda87f

———. 2016b. "Corey Lewandowski Credits FBI Director James Comey with Helping Donald Trump Win." *The Huffington Post,* November 17, 2016. http://www.huffingtonpost.com/entry/corey-lewandowski-james-comey_us_582dd4f7e4b058ce7aa97d7c

"The U.S. Illiteracy Rate Hasn't Changed in 10 Years." 2014. *The Huffington Post,* December 12, 2014. http://www.huffingtonpost.com/2013/09/06/illiteracy-rate_n_3880355.html

Tillerson, Rex W. 2017. "Remarks Addressing State Department Student Programs and Fellowship Participants." *U.S. Department of State,* August 18, 2017. https://www.state.gov/secretary/remarks/2017/08/273527.htm

"Time to Fire Trump." 2016. *The Economist,* February 27, 2016. http://www.economist.com/news/leaders/21693579-front-runner-unfit-lead-great-political-party-let-alone-america-time-fire-trump

"Top Takeaways from Nevada and South Carolina: The Secret of Trump's Media Success." 2016. *CNN's Race for the White House*, February 21, 2016. http://transcripts.cnn.com/TRANSCRIPTS/1602/21/rs.01.html

Torrenzano, Richard and Mark Davis. 2011. *Digital Assassination*. New York: St. Martin's Press.

Toynbee, Polly. 2016. "Those Out to Demonise Hillary Clinton Should Be Careful What They Wish For. *The Guardian*, June 9, 2016. https://www.theguardian.com/commentisfree/2016/jun/09/demonise-hillary-clinton-careful-us-president

Traister, Rebecca. 2017. "Hillary Clinton is Furious. And Resigned. And Funny. And Worried." *New York Magazine*, May 26, 2017. http://nymag.com/daily/intelligencer/2017/05/hillary-clinton-life-after-election.html

Traub, James. 2016. "Call It What It Is: A Rabble." *The New York Times*, March 25, 2016. http://www.nytimes.com/2016/03/27/opinion/sunday/call-it-what-it-is-a-rabble.html?

Trees, Andrew. 2016. "Founders Would Dump Trump." *USA Today*, March 31, 2016. 7A.

Troy, Gil. 2016. "And the 2016 Ralph Nader Award Goes To . . . Bernie Sanders." *Time*, November 14, 2016. http://time.com/4569766/bernie-sanders-ralph-nader-2016/

Trump, Donald. 1987, 2015. *The Art of the Deal*. New York: Ballantine.

———. 2015. "Here's Donald Trump's Presidential Announcement Speech." *Time*, June 16, 2015. http://time.com/3923128/donald-trump-announcement-speech/

———. 2016a. "Transcript of Donald Trump's Dec. 30 Speech in Hilton Head, S.C." *The Kansas City Star*, January 20, 2016. http://www.kansascity.com/news/local/news-columns-blogs/the-buzz/article55604115.html

———. 2016b. "Full Transcript of Donald Trump's Hillary Clinton Speech." *HEAVY*, June 22, 2016. http://heavy.com/news/2016/06/read-full-transcript-donald-trump-hillary-clinton-anti-speech-new-york-june-22/

———. 2016c. "Transcript: Donald J. Trump Republican Nomination Acceptance Speech." *The New York Times*, July 22, 2016. http://www.nytimes.com/2016/07/22/us/politics/trump-transcript-rnc-address.html?_r=0

———. 2016d. "Full Transcript: NYC Speech on Hillary Clinton." *Politico*, August 7, 2016. http://www.politico.com/story/2016/06/transcript-trump-speech-on-the-stakes-of-the-election-224654

———. 2016e. "Transcript of Donald Trump's Immigration Speech." *The New York Times*, September 1, 2016. https://www.nytimes.com/2016/09/02/us/politics/transcript-trump-immigration-speech.html?mcubz=3

———. 2017. "Donald Trump Twitter Post." *@realDonaldTrump*, July 1, 2017. https://twitter.com/realdonaldtrump/status/881281755017355264

"Trump's Tweets: Distracting Shiny Objects." 2017. *CNN*, August 27, 2017. http://www.cnn.com/videos/tv/2017/08/27/rs-are-trump-tweets-distracting-shiny-objects.cnn/video/playlists/reliable-sources-highlights/

Tsur, Orin, Katherine Ognyanova, and David Lazer. 2016. "The Data Behind Trump's Twitter Takeover." *Politico*, April 29, 2016. http://www.politico.com/magazine/story/2016/04/donald-trump-2016-twitter-takeover-213861

Tulis, Jeffrey. 1987. *The Rhetorical Presidency*. Princeton: Princeton University Press.

Tyson, Alec and Shiva Maniam. 2016. "Behind Trump's Victory: Divisions by Race, Gender, Education." *Pew Research Center*, November 2016. http://www.pewresearch.org/fact-tank/2016/11/09/behind-trumps-victory-divisions-by-race-gender-education/

Vanden Huevel, Katrina. 2014. "The Distorting Reality of 'False Balance' in the Media." *The Washington Post*, July 15, 2014. https://www.washingtonpost.com/opinions/katrina-vanden-heuvel-the-distorting-reality-of-false-balance-in-the-media/2014/07/14/6def5706–0b81–11e4-b8e5-d0de80767fc2_story.html?utm_term=.8564bc4807df

Vaughn, Justin. 2016. "The Post-Rhetorical Presidency of Barack Obama." *The Blue Review,* August 29, 2016. https://thebluereview.org/obama-post-rhetorical-presidency/

Vonderschmitt, Kaitlin. 2012. *The Growing Use of Social Media in Political Campaigns: How to Use Facebook, Twitter, and YouTube to Create an Effective Social Media Campaign.* Bowling Green: Western Kentucky University. http://digitalcommons.wku.edu/cgi/viewcontent.cgi?article=1366&context=stu_hon_theses

Wade, David. 2016. "Bernie Sanders, the Zombie Candidate." *Politico Magazine,* May 12, 2016. http://www.politico.com/magazine/story/2016/05/2016-primary-campaign-bernie-sanders-hillary-clinton-2004-lessons-kerry-dean-edwards-gephardt-213884

Waite, Jason. 2012. "A Review Of: Agency in the Margins: Stories of Outsider Rhetoric, Edited by Anne Meade Stockdell-Giesler." *Rhetoric Society Quarterly* 42, no. 1 (January 10, 2012): 94–97.

Waldman, Paul. 2015. "Donald Trump is Now Running the Most Explicitly Racist Campaign Since 1968." *The Week,* November 25, 2015. http://theweek.com/articles/590711/donald-trump-running-most-explicitly-racist-campaign-since-1968

———. 2016. "Trump's White Supremacist Tweets Aren't the Problem. They're a Symptom of the Problem." *The Washington Post,* July 4, 2016. https://www.washingtonpost.com/blogs/plum-line/wp/2016/07/04/trumps-white-supremacist-tweets-arent-the-problem-theyre-a-symptom-of-the-problem/?post-share=1791467673577427&tid=ss_fb-bottom

Wallis, Jim. 2016. "It's Embarrassing to be an Evangelical This Election." *Soujourners,* February 25, 2016. https://sojo.net/articles/it-s-embarrassing-be-evangelical-election

Wang, Sam. 2016. "The Comey Effect." *Princeton Election Consortium,* December 10, 2016. http://election.princeton.edu/2016/12/10/the-comey-effect

Ward, Lucas. 2017. "Professors Debate Future of Democracy at IOP." *The Harvard Crimson,* September 5, 2017. http://www.thecrimson.com/article/2017/9/6/iop-democracy-peril/

Warren, James. 2016. "Fall of the House of Bush." *U.S. News and World Report,* February 17, 2016. http://www.usnews.com/opinion/articles/2016-02-17/2016-anti-establishment-rage-may-betray-jeb-and-bush-family-legacy

Wehner, Peter. 2016. "The Indelible Stain of Donald Trump." *The New York Times,* June 10, 2016. http://www.nytimes.com/2016/06/12/opinion/campaign-stops/the-indelible-stain-of-donald-trump.html?smid=fb-nytimes&smtyp=cur

Weiss, Joanna. 2012. "Partisan Politics: Take a Look at the 19th Century." *The Boston Globe,* October 9, 2012. https://www.bostonglobe.com/opinion/2012/10/08/partisan-politics-take-look-century/04FsP1WkuqPNEUioPSqpUP/story.html

Weiss, Max. 2016. "Things I Blame for Hillary Clinton's Loss, Ranked." *The Huffington Post,* December 5, 2016. http://www.huffingtonpost.com/entry/things-i-blame-for-hillary-clintons-loss-ranked_us_58459894e4b0496fbcb0c26d

Wendling, Mike. 2016. "Trump's Shock Troops: Who Are the 'Alt-Right'?" *BBC News,* August 26, 2016. http://www.bbc.com/news/magazine-37021991

Wertheim, L. Jon, and Sam Sommers. 2016. "The Eternal Appeal of the Underdog." *The New York Times,* March 15, 2016. http://www.nytimes.com/2016/03/15/opinion/the-eternal-appeal-of-the-underdog.html

West, Sarrell and Johanna Dunaway. 2017. *Mass Media and American Politics.* Washington, D.C.: CQ Press.

White, Zachery. 2003. "Re-Examining Kenneth Burke on 'Identification' in the 'New' Rhetoric." PhD diss., Purdue University. http://docs.lib.purdue.edu/dissertations/AAI3113888/

Wickens, Mary. 2016. "Letter to the Editor." *The New York Times,* June 29, 2016. http://www.nytimes.com/2016/06/30/opinion/dear-bernie-sanders-what-you-didnt-say.html?smid=fb-share

Will, George. 2014. "George Will: The Price of Political Ignorance." *The Washington Post,* January 1, 2014. https://www.washingtonpost.com/opinions/george-will-the-

price-of-political-ignorance/2014/01/01/7dbe2936–7311–11e3–9389–09ef9944065e_
story.html?utm_term=.e76b613987f0

Williams, Joseph. 2017. "Democrats' Race Problem." *US News and World Report*, August 11, 2017. https://www.usnews.com/news/the-report/articles/2017–08–11/democrats-face-a-rift-in-their-own-party-over-race

Williams, Ray. 2014. "The Cult of Ignorance in the United States: Anti-Intellectualism and the 'Dumbing Down' of America." *Psychology Today*, June 7, 2014. https://www.sott.net/article/313177-The-cult-of-ignorance-in-the-United-States-Anti-intellectualism-and-the-dumbing-down-of-America

Williamson, Kevin D. 2016. "Our Government Was Designed to Protect Us from the Trumps of the World." *National Review*, March 18, 2016. http://www.nationalreview.com/article/432941/donald-trump-populist-demagogue-john-adams-anticipated

Wilts, Alexandria. 2017. "Donald Trump Claims Putin Would Have Preferred if Hillary Clinton Was President." *Independent*, July 12, 2017. http://www.independent.co.uk/news/world/americas/us-politics/trump-putin-clinton-prefer-president-us-election-win-cbn-interview-a7838396.html

Wodak, Ruth. 2015. *The Politics of Fear: What Right-Wing Populist Discourses Mean*. New York: Sage.

Woffard, Taylor. 2015. "Donald Trump Talks Like a 4th Grader: Report." *Newsweek*, August 14, 2015. http://www.newsweek.com/donald-trump-hello-you-people-know-lot-about-trucks-363077

Womack, Larry. 2016. "Dear Bernie: I Like You, But These Red Flags Are Too Frequent To Ignore." *The Huffington Post*, February 23, 2016. http://www.huffingtonpost.com/larry-womack/dear-bernie-red-flags-frequent_b_9289954.html

Wood, Peregrin. 2015. "Transcript of the Bernard Sanders 2016 Presidential Announcement Speech." *Irregular Times*, April 20, 2015. http://irregulartimes.com/2015/04/30/transcript-of-the-bernard-sanders-2016-presidential-announcement-speech/

Woodruff, Betsy. 2016. "Coal Country Loves Coal-Hating Bernie Sanders." *The Daily Beast*, May 5, 2016. http://www.thedailybeast.com/articles/2016/05/05/coal-country-loves-coal-hating-bernie-sanders.html

Zakaria, Fareed. 2016. "Transcript: GPS." *CNN.com*, March 13, 2016. http://transcripts.cnn.com/TRANSCRIPTS/1603/13/fzgps.01.html

Zompetti, Joseph P. 2015. *Divisive Discourse: The Extreme Rhetoric of Contemporary American Politics*. San Diego: Carnella Academic Publishing.

Index

About the Author

Colleen Elizabeth Kelley is associate professor of rhetorical communication at Penn State Erie, The Behrend College. Dr. Kelley holds a PhD in rhetorical theory and criticism from the University of Oregon. Her previous books include *Post-9/11 American Presidential Rhetoric: A Study of Protofascist Discourse* and *The Rhetoric of First Lady Hillary Rodham Clinton: Crisis Management Discourse.*

Lightning Source UK Ltd.
Milton Keynes UK
UKOW04n1531040218
317350UK00001B/6/P